THE ✦ NEW ✦ AGE
COMMUNITY GUIDEBOOK

Alternative Choices in Lifestyles

- Community Directory Listings

- Community Articles

- Resources

HARBIN SPRINGS PUBLISHING

Fourth Edition, Revised

This book is manufactured in the United States of America.
Front cover art is by George D'Elena, P. O. Box 782, Middletown, CA 95461; Back cover art by Wahaba Heartsun, P. O. Box 1084, Cottage Grove, OR 97424.

First Printing 1985 was published by Community Referral Service, Box 2672, Eugene, OR 97402.
Second Printing 1986, revised, was published by Janes Publishing, 25671 Fleck Rd., Veneta, OR 97487.
Third Printing 1988, revised, was published by Janes Publishing, 25671 Fleck Rd., Veneta, OR 97487.
Fourth Printing 1989, revised, was published by Harbin Springs Publishing, P. O. Box 82, Middletown, CA 95461

Second Printing revised edition Library of Congress Card Catalog Number: 86-83137
Third Printing revised edition Library of Congress Card Catalog Number: 88-
The New Age Community Guidebook - Alternative Choices in Lifestyles
Fourth Printing revised edition Library of Congress Card Catalog Number: 89-11073
The New Age Community Guidebook - Alternative Choices in Lifestyles

Second Printing revised edition ISBN 0-938333-17-8
Third Printing revised edition ISBN 0-938333-09-7
Fourth Printing revised edition ISBN 0-944202-03-9

Dear Friends,

The information in this book has been collected in an attempt to assist those who are interested in alternative lifestyles, serving those already living "in community" as well as those who are investigating available options for a future community living experience.

This book would not have been possible without the help of all those community members who submitted articles, photos, and listings for the directory. Thanks so much to all of you! You made this book what it is. You did the hard part. All I did was put it together in a cohesive manner.

This book is for you, the community-minded--the people who are looking for a better, more supportive, more conscious lifestyle. Here on these pages you will find thousands of other people, like yourself, who are taking responsibility for making a change in their lives and in the world.

I hope you enjoy the guidebook, as well as find it useful and informative. I welcome any ideas, comments or feedback.

Peace,

Libby S. Baltrusch
Editor

ARTWORK CREDITS:
Artwork on pages 5, 57 and 115
by George D'Elena

Artwork on pages 15, 48, 51, 66, 85 and 107
by Wahaba Heartsun

TABLE OF CONTENTS

General Articles

A CHECKLIST FOR THOSE WANTING TO JOIN COMMUNITIES

by Corinne McLaughlin and Gordon Davidson

Are you wondering if you're a community person? Do you think you would fit in with a community? No matter who you are, the answer is probably yes, as there's undoubtedly a community somewhere for every type of person. However, here are a few qualities which are generally needed in most communities, so you can see how you'd fare in one:

1. A willingness to think and act in terms of the good of the whole, not just in terms of personal needs and opinions--in other words, good old-fashioned unselfishness (or at least a willingness to grow in this direction).

2. Tolerance for differences and open-mindedness towards different points of view.

3. A willingness to work out conflicts and not hold grudges, with a realistic belief in the possibility of resolving differences to mutual satisfaction.

4. A somewhat adventurous and courageous spirit, open to change, flexible and adaptable.

5. A generally social nature--liking to be with people much of the time (hermit types would climb the wall!).

Although perfection in all of these qualities is hardly expected (and rarely achieved), a willingness to change and grow into these qualities *is* important.

How would you know if community living was right for you, even if you had the above qualities? What should you look for in a community? This depends on what your personal values are. Here are some things you might want to explore and reflect on as you read about the various communities or explore and visit them:

1. If you are mainly looking for a supportive and loving environment with lots of good friends, then spend as much time as you can with members of the community on a one-to-one basis, getting to know them personally to determine if you have an easy and natural harmony with them. If you don't feel a good heart-to-heart connection with them at first, it may be more difficult to become close friends later. Even though they may be good people, you may not have a basic "resonance" with each other on a personality level, even though you may share common ideals and values. So if support and nurturance are highest on your agenda, relative to other values listed here, then this may not be your "family". Also, observe how much time members hang out with each other, have social activities like parties or sports together, if an active social life is what you're interested in. Check out how much harmony or conflict there is among members, and feel out the "vibes"--the general atmosphere--of the community when you first arrive. Your intuition will tell you whether this is "home" for you.

2. If spirituality is the most important value for you, then find out what the common beliefs and practices of the community are. Are these in harmony with your own? Are there regular meditation or prayer times, study groups, yoga practices, a library of spiritual books available for reading? Are the spiritual practices required of members, or are they left up to individual choice? Are they fairly structured or unstructured? If practices are not required or structured, ask yourself whether you have the necessary self-discipline to choose to do them, or do you require help with this. If you need some kind of authority structure or guru, are you ready to submit to it and not express rebelliousness? Also, notice what happens day to day in community life. Do members actually work at *living* their spiritual beliefs? Do they inspire you? Is the general atmosphere uplifting and positive? Although many communities proclaim similar spiritual ideals--love, sharing, brother/sisterhood, you have to actually spend time in each community to see how it works out in practice.

3. If equality and shared governance and decision-making are most important to you, then you should explore how power and leadership actually function in the community. Go beyond the theory and the words and look at the practice. Are there any authoritarian leaders or dependent, subservient followers? Who really makes the major decisions? By what process? How involved is the whole membership in decision-making? Is there openness to feedback in the leadership? Are members taking their fair share of responsibility, or leaving it to a few others? How decentralized is power in the community?

4. If economic equality and sharing of resources is most important, then note how income is made and where it goes. Is income pooled and all bills paid out of a common pot, or is income individually kept? Is everyone required to work an equal amount of time? Is all work equally shared and valued--including things like cleaning and childcare? How are land, houses, vehicles, machinery and other resources owned--communally or individually--or, is there some mix of communal/individual? If income and resources are more individual, how do members feel about this? Is there resentment or acceptance?

5. If privacy and individual freedom are highest on your list, then check out housing and financial arrangements. Does everyone live in one big house, or are there individual dwellings? Are these privately or communally-owned? If houses are shared, are bedrooms and/or other spaces in the house designated as private? How

well sound-proofed are shared houses? Are they quiet enough when needed? Are all meals communal, or are some or all meals individual? Is there personal choice of lifestyle, or does everyone have to live the same way? Does everyone have the same spiritual and political values, or is there room for diversity? How much time and work energy are required for membership? How many required meetings are there?

6. If "living lightly on the earth"--a simple lifestyle with appropriate technology, organic gardening, recycling--is what you most desire, explore how homes are built and how they are heated. How many appliances are there, how many (if any) TV's, etc. How is kitchen and other waste used--is it recycled into compost? Is food home-grown and organic or is it store-bought? How vital and productive is the garden? Are furniture, clothing, equipment, tools, etc. mostly new or recycled (used)? How extensively is wind or solar energy used?

7. If feminist values are most important to you, then find out who does what jobs in the community. Do men share cooking, cleaning, childcare? Are women working in administrative and leadership positions and sharing heavier work like construction and mechanics? How is sexuality viewed in the community? Are there a majority of celibates in the community? Or families? Or singles? Gays? Are women's opinions as highly valued in the community as men's?

Are certain behaviors deemed more appropriate for one sex or the other, or is there freedom of expression?

8. If a supportive and safe environment for children and/or shared childcare are what you're most looking for, then observe who has responsibility for children--individual parents, or the whole community (or somewhere in between)? Notice also whether childcare is structured or informal, and whether there are good teachers and schools in the community or nearby. Are there reasonably-sized accommodation spaces available in the community or nearby for families? How much time commitment is asked of community members, and does this leave time for family? What are the trade-offs between a totally nuclear family setting and community? Are there children of similar age for playing with? Are there community playgrounds or spaces just for children? Is there a general sense of happiness and harmony among families?

No community is a utopia, and none will offer the ideal arrangements in all these areas. Each community has its special focus, based on its own values and philosophy But if you find a community you really like, but are disappointed that it's not living up to something that you feel is important, then perhaps it is a message to you to do something *yourself* to change or improve it, rather than criticize it. It's easy to throw stones from the sidelines. It's harder--and yet more rewarding--to create something better, and so give a gift to all those who will come later to the community. And, if you find that no community seems to live up to your ideals, then perhaps it's best to turn within and ask whether you are living these ideals yourself, as maybe you are searching in vain for something outside yourself that can really only be found within. Perhaps this is the place to begin.

(© copyright 1985. Reprinted with permission from Corinne McLaughlin)

THE "FLOWER CHILDREN" COME OF AGE

by Joy Foster

What has happened to the flower children of the sixties and seventies? Some have continued in a rebellious withdrawal from mainstream society; others have left that experience behind and rejoined society to become successful in the traditional way. But a third element has "come of age in the mature assumption of responsibility as global citizens", says Dave Thatcher of 100 Mile House. A product of the sixties himself, Thatcher has travelled and lectured widely in the Western world, becoming an authority on the "New Age" movement and intentional communities.

"As individuals and communities many of us have left behind our childish reactionary tendencies," he said in an interview with *Integrity International*. "We no longer speak of ourselves as an "alternative society" but as "complementary catalysts" or "centers of light".

"Many communities now operate schools, businesses, counselling and medical practices--not only as a means of providing economic sustenance but more essentially as an avenue of blessing and creative assistance to a very needy world. And as this expansive maturity continues, we find ourselves meeting one another as co-creators of a harmonious planet Earth."

In the process of maturing many are shifting their approach from one of confrontation over issues such as nuclear arms and environmental protection to one of respecting and working with existing authorities. "I have met many people in positions of leadership in the world," said Thatcher, "and without exception all have been concerned with peace and are pursuing it to the highest of their vision and capability. We as their progeny defeat ourselves if we react to what they are providing rather than offering our complementary vision from a position of understanding and respect."

Thatcher cited the example of a friend who was helping organize the Seabrook nuclear power plant protest in New Jersey two years ago.

"The organizers were planning a Gandhi-type protest and expected to be carted off to jail," he said. "I suggested that although Gandhi's approach was useful a few decades ago, time has moved on and something new was needed. Why not rent gasoline generators and coffee urns, buy donuts and invite the Nuclear Regulatory Commission authorities, the Project Superintendent and their associates and employees to confer over coffee in a field by the construction site, and express our point of view from a stance of genuine respect?"

This was done and as it turned out the project was terminated a year later.

David Thatcher, expert on the "New Age" movement and intentional communities has authored a book entitled *Earthrise - A Personal Responsibility*.

"At a surface glance one wouldn't see any connection between this meeting and the ultimate termination of the project," said Thatcher, "but my impression is that we are beginning to see the operation of a certain magic here. Because these people were willing to confer as friends, the NRC as time continued, saw a number of factors come before them that indicated they needed to shut down the plant."

"This kind of approach has been gaining momentum," he continued. "I receive a number of newsletters put out by people concerned with nuclear energy and I've noted since this event emphasis being put on being for life rather than against nuclear development, on coming from a place of peace and harmony within oneself. This is not a position of weakness but one of great flexibility and strength."

It comes back to the individual's personal experience.

As an example closer to home, Thatcher has lived in the Emissary community at 100 Mile House for fourteen years. He found himself having to work with a person who tended to speak to him in an abrasive and overbearing way.

"So I thought about him in quiet times," he said, "recognizing the idiosyncrasies which were there but deliberately looking at aspects of this man which were

David Thatcher, noted author and expert on the "New Age"

worthy of my respect and support. As I generated this appreciation the other aspects tended to diminish in my consciousness."

"Naturally I had the opportunity to prove this out a few days later. He approached me with his habitual stance and delivered his diatribe, but this time there was no reaction in me. We were looking eye to eye, and within seconds he recognized the absurdity of his expression and we embraced. That opened a whole new chapter in our developing friendship."

In the growth of intentional communities, Thatcher has noted certain cycles.

Out of approximately 100,000 communities begun in North America in the past two decades, about 3,000 are still functioning, he reports. Those that have persisted, he feels, have done so because they have taken spiritual values into account, rather than being preoccupied with physical concerns such as growing organic food or escaping from the cities.

"One of the reasons for the breakdown of some communities has been the inability or unwillingness of the leadership to let their members mature and share increasing responsibility for the government of the community as time went on" he said.

Thatcher also maintains that, while it is often denied, there is always a point of leadership in a successful community, however quietly the person operates.

In a recent tour of Australia and New Zealand, he found that the same counter-culture movement that was sweeping America 10 or 15 years ago has been sweeping Australia. His experience and vision were welcomed warmly and he found himself with more invitations to speak and appear on the media than he could possibly handle. He was interviewed on "Good Morning Australia," which is televised nationwide, and featured in a six-page color spread in Australia's leading alternative magazine, *Simply Living*. He was also asked by the Australian Broadcasting Company to be a consultant for a worldwide six-part series on cooperative lifestyles.

During his tour, Thatcher discovered that Australian Prime Minister Bob Hawke is particularly interested in communal living situations, especially for the young and unemployed. His daughter has been in Japan studying communes there and he had also sent a cabinet minister to Israel to study kibbutzim.

Thatcher believes that a new wave of interest in communal living is underway in North America. This is evidenced through features in the Denver *Post* about Sunrise Ranch in Colorado and the Boston *Globe's* interview with Corinne McLaughlin and Gordon Davidson.

Even the Wall Street Journal presented an article on spiritual and communal groups in the United States.

While he feels communities play a special role, "like greenhouses, nurturing a new complementary lifestyle," he certainly doesn't suggest that everyone needs to live in a community in order to find themselves, or that they are a universal panacea. He often says in his lectures that what he is most interested in is the spirit of community.

"Humanity is crossing a threshold from the Industrial Age into a time which necessitates a new spirit of global cooperation," he says, "This recognition is coming in every field, and comes to a certain focus in the communal groups themselves, where there has been an accelerating reaching out and working together as a family of friends."

Providing a means for this collective interaction are emerging networks such as the Earth Community Network, the New England Network of Light, the Fellowship of Intentional Communities and the Stewardship of Communities.

Observing the present order of things in the Western and Communist societies, Thatcher had this comment to make:

"Since the 1950's we have been carrying out an anti-communist vendetta in the West. It appears to me that we are reacting to what we conceive to be the communist undermining of the creative potential and responsibility of the individual, with the state declaring itself to be the whole meaning and purpose of one's life. On the other hand, the egocentricity and sense of isolation which manifests in the free enterprise system as 'doing your own thing' is equally ludicrous. We need to leave behind both these concepts about collective human function and discover our inherent complementary reality. As we reawaken to this already-present spiritual identity, the new forms of our creative interaction will naturally emerge step by step."

Thatcher's book, *Earthrise: A Personal Responsibility* presents an overview to the unprecedented change sweeping the planet. It is based on his 20 years experience of living with over 100 others on a British Columbia ranch and consciousness and social change worldwide.

Article reprinted with permission from Integrity International, Box 9, 100 Mile House, B.C. VOK 2EO. For information on Integrity International see the Resource section of this publication.

FEDERATION OF EGALITARIAN COMMUNITIES
by Laird Sandhill

COMMUNITIES IN DIALOGUE:

APPLETREE COMMUNITY
P. O. Box 5
Cottage Grove, OR 97424
(503) 942-4372

DANDELION COMMUNITY
R.R. 1
Enterprise, Ontario
CANADA K0K 1Z0
(613) 358-2304

EAST WIND COMMUNITY
Box 6B2
Tucumseh, MO 65760
(417) 679-4682

METTANOKIT COMMUNITY
Another Place
Rt. 123
Greenville, NH 03048
(603) 878-3117

SANDHILL FARM
Rt. 1, Box 155
Rutledge, MO 63563
(816) 883-5543

TWIN OAKS COMMUNITY
Rt. 4, Box 169
Louisa, VA 23093
(703) 894-5126

FOUNDATION FOR FEEDBACK LEARNING
139 Corson Ave.
Staten Island, NY 10301
(718) 720-5378

KRUTSIO COMMUNITY
Apdo Postal 2228
Ensenada, Baja California
Mexico 22800

SPRINGTREE COMMUNITY
Rt. 2, Box 89
Scottsville, VA 24590
(804) 286-3466

A little more than ten years ago, five North American communities shared a dream of cooperation. As a result, representatives of these communities got together in 1976 and founded the Federation of Egalitarian Communities. Since then the Federation has been evolving and maturing, realizing some of the original dreams and fostering new ones.

Today there are six member communities (Appletree, Dandelion, East Wind, Mettanokit, Sandhill Farm, and Twin Oaks) and three groups affiliated as communities-in-dialogue (Foundation for Feedback Learning, Krutsio and Springtree). All together about 200 people are represented by these nine communities. Our combined businesses gross about one million dollars annually.

The Federation is growing. Perhaps you or your community could grow with us. Each Federation community makes its own selections on individuals. To be a member of the Federation, each community must:

1) hold its land, labor and other resources in common;
2) assume responsibility for the needs of its members, distributing all goods and services equally, or according to need;
3) practice non-violence;
4) use a form of decision-making in which members have an equal opportunity to participate either through consensus, direct vote or right of appeal or overrule;
5) work to establish equality of all people and not permit discrimination on the basis of race, class, creed, ethnic origin, age, sex, or sexual orientation;
6) act to conserve natural resources for present and future generations while striving to continually improve ecological awareness and practice;
7) create processes for group communication and participation and provide an environment which supports people's development.

What are the Benefits of Membership?

Recruitment

The Federation has worked hardest to provide its members with support in the area of recruitment and outreach. This support takes many forms. Every year we place at least $2,000 worth of print ads in alternative periodicals, generating hundreds of responses.

To answer these inquiries, we have put together an introductory brochure describing all the member communities in detail. Today, whenever a letter of inquiry comes into one community, information about all our communities goes out.

its spirit and benefit from it. This attempt to go beyond the present state of humanity is, in fact, a call for a new world.

Auroville International, a registered international body, has its main office in Holland and its secretariat in Paris. It has members in most parts of the world and centers in Holland, France, USA, Canada, Sweden, Italy, Germany, Switzerland, and the United Kingdom. These centers are bases of support for and information on Auroville.

Child's Garden
A Community For Our Children
For The Children Inside Us All
And For The Children Of Our World

We call it Child's Garden because, for us, we come together, most of all, to help each other provide for our children the kind of truly nurturing, empowering and joyous beginnings that might make it possible for them to become all that their hearts and souls would long for them to be.

We call it Child's Garden because we believe that there are no more important years in our entire lifetimes than the first ones, that it is during these years we learn whether or not life is to be trusted, whether or not other people are to be trusted, and whether or not we can trust ourselves. And so we feel it is very important to nurture and honor and protect our children during these early years.

We call it Child's Garden because, for us, children represent the very essence of human nature—the feelings and needs and instincts and impulses and desires of human nature—which our civilization has, for milleniums, feared and believed need to be overcome, tamed, brought under control. We believe, to the contrary, that our very deepest instincts are loving and cooperative ones, and that, if children feel truly loved and safe and free to be themselves, they will become more kind and caring and cooperative than any of us have ever become through efforts made to mold and control us. We come together to create the kind of loving environment which will show that to be true, which will provide a model of how all children might be in a truly loving world.

We call it Child's Garden because we believe that it is during childhood that nearly all of us in this civilization substantially lose ourselves; and that only by reclaiming the feelings and needs we learned to deny in our childhoods, only by reclaiming that child buried inside us, will we become whole again.

We call it Child's Garden because we believe that it is crucial, in this time when all life on our planet is so much at risk, that we learn how to trust the human nature which children represent, that we learn how to heal the children inside nearly all of us that have become so deeply distrustful and that we learn how to trust and honor and protect our children so that they might grow to be the kind of people who will truly create peace on this earth, an Eden which our race has always sensed ought to be and could be our true home.

We call it Child's Garden because, for us, it is the nurturing and honoring and protecting of our children (and the healing of the children inside ourselves and each other) that we feel to be our most sacred task; and that it is the process of awakening and opening and yielding and surrendering—which this task so continually requires of us—which we see as our most sacred, daily, ongoing spiritual practice. It is often not an easy path. And that is especially why we are so much in need of each other's support, inspiration, camaraderie, and deep and close friendship.

Child's Garden is a community about to be born. If what we have shared here touches your heart, speaks to your most sacred longings and ideals, we invite you to consider joining us in giving birth to this community. There are, of course, a great many practical considerations not explored here. Though we have already explored many of these and feel strong leanings in certain directions, we feel that it is only together—with the input and sharing of all those who would make Child's Garden their own—that all these details shall be decided.

For more information about Child's Garden and/or to share your responses, please write to Gary and Carole Sugarman, 2228 S. El Camino Real, #14, San Mateo, CA 94403 or call (415) 341-2852.

BREITENBUSH COMMUNITY
Breitenbush Hot Springs Retreat and Conference Center

P. O. Box 578
Detroit, OR 97342
503-854-3314

In the heart of the Breitenbush River Drainage is a place long held sacred as healing land by Native Americans. In this place 40 - 60 hot springs bubble to the surface. Each has a different mineral content and many became famous in the first half of the century for their specific healing qualities. The hot springs resort built in the 1920's and 30's eventually was sold, and in the 1960's fell into ruin. In 1977 a young man with a vision bought the old resort.

After four years of hard work by Alex, his wife Peggy, and the friends who gathered around them, they were able to once again reopen the land to guests. They had restored 40 guest cabins, rebuilt the hydro-electric plant and flume, drilled deep wells and, with heat exchangers designed by themselves, begun to heat the buildings geothermally. The work has continued with restoration of the beautiful old lodge, care of the many springs, and construction of hot water facilities for guests.

The Community has grown to 30 adults and 5 children, people whose common vision is to act as stewards of this very special place so that groups and individuals may share in the healing of the land and water. Guests are invited to join community members in early morning meditation and yoga in the new sanctuary. For soaking and steaming we have our Medicine Wheel hot tubs, natural rock-lined pools in the meadow and the steam sauna. We have a work exchange program available by prior arrangement so that more people can participate in community life.

The issues we face as a community are complicated mixtures of business, community and personality. Presently, Breitenbush is a worker-owned and operated business. In addition, we work to preserve the beautiful Old Growth Cathedral Forest which lies around our land. Much of this virgin forest is scheduled for logging. For example, Devils' Ridge is an untouched area scheduled for several timber sales and road building. When we stand on our footbridge over the Breitenbush River we look upstream to this ridge (see photo). We have been working with conservationists and friends, particularly the Oregon Natural Resources Council, in the forest-planning process of our Willamette National Forest. We want to encourage people to use the network of trails connecting Breitenbush to the Mt. Jefferson Wilderness Area, both for hiking and cross-country skiing. We are currently involved in litigation against the U.S. Government over their policies of timber management. Our community is united by our love of these lands and waters and our commitment to service. Beyond that we are very diverse in our personal philosophies and goals. We invite people to come visit. Please contact us for information, rates and workshop schedules. We require reservations to insure all our guests the finest quality stay. Thank you.

Devil's Ridge as seen from the footbridge

THE BUILDERS

Box 2121
Oasis, NV 89835-2121
(702) 478-5112

The Builders derives its name from the ancient ones referred to in Genesis as the Sons of God, who were on earth before the creation of man. These beings are Christ Conscious entities, responsible for the evolution of lifeforms in the expanding spheres of creation. The Builders of old and of present are the evolution of the true Sons and Daughters of Divine Spirit.

The world we know is being transformed by an evolution of consciousness that is pressing in upon us, changing us forever. Each spirit is divine and immortal; all who choose are going to experience this, growing into a love we have only glimpsed.

The Builders are souls united to facilitate this enlightenment. The group began in the late 1960's. A core of about 100 men and women has remained together since 1972.

Meditation

Norman Paulsen, the founder of The Builders, received a meditation technique from Paramahansa Yogananda that allowed him to achieve his greatest desire,"....to find and meet God," (described in his book, *Christ Consciousness*). Brother Norman experienced our Divine Creator in its favorite manifestation, a living, loving, sphere of brilliant Light. This consciousness wants to share itself with all humanity, and is available to whomever is willing to receive.

The new age we are entering is one of knowing, not just believing. "To as many as would receive gave He the power to become the sons and daughters of God," full participants and co-creators. Those who practice the SUN meditation technique with sincere devotion, discipline and dedication can meet God face to face, and can experience the reality of our true immortal nature. Direct Divine guidance and daily contact with the Creator are possible through the use of this tool.

Community

Unprecendented spiritual growth is possible at this time. Mother/Father/God is communicating with millions of people on this planet through direct and immediate personal experiences. If you have not already, you can encounter this great Being of Light and Love.

The dawning of the cosmic sense brings with it the understanding that we are all one; each face is our own. A united world community needs to work together to heal itself and our Mother, the Earth. We can build this unity by starting with ourselves.

The Builders are souls consciously striving to enter enlightenment, the next step in man's evolution. Association with like minded souls is one of the greatest means to this end. This and our meditation tool are our strongest assets.

Our association with each other is a powerful magnet for receiving Christ Consciousness. Individually and as a group, Builders meditate daily using the Sun Meditation Technique. Each strives to incorporate the twelve virtues and eight paths into daily life, and to donate 10% of income and/or services to The Builders' non-profit organization.

We are a do-it-yourself group. There is no formal membership and no membership committee. You are free to choose this way of life, or association with those who have choosen the way of The Builders. Most important is your own commitment to, and relationship with the Divine Creator, to live in a manner which supports and stregthens this inner bond.

All Builders manage their own income and expenses. Some work for Builder-owned businesses, some own their own businesses; others are employed elsewhere.

Visitors are welcome at any of our centers, to our daily meditations and other events. Contact the following for schedule and to visit:

All Correspondence should be addressed to the Nevada center: Dawn King at Box 2121, Oasis, NV 89835-2121, (702) 478-5112.

In Utah contact Jonathan and Valerie King at our Clearbrook Center, 576 E. Vine #3B, Salt Lake City, UT 84107.

In California contact The Sojourn at Vintage Marina, 2950 S. Harbor Blvd., Oxnard, CA 93030, (805) 985-6417

In Arizona contact David & Diane Eddy at the New Frontiers Natural Foods Store (formerly Winnies), Flagstaff, AZ, (602) 527-0334.

"Life outside a person is an extension of the life within him. This compels him to be part of it and accept responsibility for all creatures great and small. Life becomes harder when we live for others but it also becomes richer and happier."--Albert Schweitzer

CASA MARIA (House of Mary)
Catholic Worker House of Hospitality

1131 N. 21st St.
P. O. Box 05206
Milwaukee, WI 53205

Casa Maria is a Catholic Worker house based on the philosophy of non-violence, poverty and helping those in need. The house was started in 1967 by Mike and Netty Cullen and family with the help of other people who saw the need of the Catholic Church to become more involved in helping the poor on the streets. The house is large enough to house four families, three single women and three community members. The families and single women stay with us until they find another place to live.

The community gives out food to the hungry and clothes and used furniture to those in need. The community also works for justice and peace on the local, national and international level. The community, at present, is composed of 25 people from various walks of life who take care of the house and its activities. Any one can help with the house provided they are non-violent and have a sincere spirit of caring for people. None of us who work at the house are paid for the work we do here since it is done in the Christian conviction that we should take care of our sisters and brothers in need without seeking any reward for this.

The community prays together each Wednesday evening at 7 p.m. in order to get strength and spiritual nourishment so we can continue our work of healing and caring. On Sunday evening the community gets together to discuss business of the house and plan for any events taking place in the following week. This is also the time when new people who want to join our community can introduce themselves and express their interest in the house and its activities.

Our community is interested in rooting out the violence in our society and the causes of hunger and homelessness. As a result we do not cooperate with the governments of this country and its system. We sometimes go to jail for speaking out against violence, especially that of the military, and other unjust institutions that we see in our midst. We try to be as personal as possible with all people. We do not want our house to become like a hotel or an agency, but a home for our guests. We do what we feel the Gospel directs us to do, and we do it only for that reason.

Our house is maintained by the members of our community and by people who want to support our efforts. We receive no funding from the Church, government or any corporation. We choose not to receive money from these institutions since we would be restricted in our efforts to resist violence and take care of the needy. We do not choose to be tax exempt because we do not want any special favors for doing what we are doing, we do not want to cooperate with a violent system and we want to be more unified with the poor who receive no special exemptions for what they do for others.

We publish a monthly newsletter called *Casa Cry* which is sent for free to whomever wishes to receive it. It keeps people informed on what we are doing here and how they can get involved with our activities.

We are always looking for new members for our community since the more people we have in the community the more we can do for the needy and the more we can try to root out the causes of such poverty.

We ask for your prayers, your involvement and your support in our work.

CHILDREN OF THE LIGHT

The Manifestation of the Family of God

Star Rt. Box 39
Dateland, AZ 85333

We, the Children of Light, were supernaturally chosen and called out in 1949, by God sending the Risen Christ Jesus in His Visible Presence into our midst, and He has remained with us ever since. He called us out of man's natural way of living as the families of man, to live as the Family of God, providing the way for us to live as manifested Sons of God, the same way as that One Son of Man, Jesus Christ, lived--wholly under Spirit-control for food, drink and raiment, and all our daily actions. This is God's Way to redeem the body from death. "If the Spirit of Him that raised up Jesus from the dead dwell in you, He that raised up Christ from the dead shall also quicken your mortal bodies by His Spirit that dwelleth in you." (Romans 8:11)

Through the power of this Divine Visitation from God, we are living the fulfillment of Jesus' words, of selling all possessions to have all in common, forsaking all flesh relations, and living "as eunuchs and virgins for the Kingdom of Heaven's sake." As Jesus said: "If a man keeps My sayings, he shall never see (experience) death." (Mark 10:21, Matt. 19:12, 29; John 8:51.) Death is the last enemy to be overcome and destroyed, and it can only be overcome by a body of people letting God have His headship or command over them; letting Him be their Father, even as He is the Father of Jesus Christ.

This is the most serious hour in the entire history of the world, for the signs all declare that this is the time of the end on God's clock, for man's natural way of living, which is the foundation of this world's system, under the god of money. God has decreed the awesome destruction of this world's system, which Jesus declared in Matt. 24:21, 22: "For then shall be great tribulation, such as was not since the beginning of the world to this time, no, nor ever shall be again. And except those days should be shortened, there should no flesh be saved; but for the sake of the Elect those days shall be shortened."

God promised that He would not let all flesh be destroyed, so He has prepared a place of safety, where He can hide and protect His own from the coming storm. His Ark for today is a body of people under the Mind of Christ, living in a place where whosoever will can come and live Jesus' Way with the Family of God, which gives Jesus Christ His Kingdom on Earth.

The place that He has provided is on 80 acres of land, a beautiful oasis in the desert, with an abundance of water, three wells, two with windmills and water tanks, and two generator plants for electricity, and with huge shade trees, over 100 date palms, and other fruit trees. There is also a large main building with assembly room, dining room, kitchen, dormitory and sleeping rooms, sewing room and patios, as well as several other buildings, including laundry, storehouses and trailers. This is God's provision for His own in this end time, and all are welcome to "come and see" what great things the Lord has done, whereof we are glad.

CHRISTMAS STAR

c/o Wind Spirit
2300 Dripping Springs Road
Winkelman, AZ 85292
(213) 280-9992

Healing and transforming, developing, self-reliant survival-oriented land base, small and growing, is reaching to connect with serious future builders working for the great plan to provide ways to help others to treat the earth as sacred, the animals as friends and helpers, and other beings as precious.

The 50 acres of subtropical Arizona desert mountain wilderness sits in a fertile valley that offers an abundant environment for the many varieties of fruit trees, plants, and untapped cottage industry potentials. There are small dome housing structures, a ranch house, spa and bathing area, tool and equipment facilities, irrigated orchards and vineyards, and many other projects in the making. Residents and friends help with new projects, caretake the land and share utilities. Children are warmly welcome as well as horses and other non-neurotic animals.

"The vision that launched this movement was one of completion, perfection, ecstatic reunion, home and communion."

The foundation of the vision began in Los Angeles with a small group of people forming the Academy of Atlantis. From this circle of light the magnet drew others to come and ignite their visions conjunctively. Christmas Star was born out of this collaboration to be a future survival base to rejuvenate souls and house a way to allow the mission to continue during periods of great upheavals and crisis. It is a haven to provide the protection and energy of trees and plants, the smell of the Earth, nurturing and sustenance for our souls

and a place to restore faith. The Atlantis Circle of Light is the business and creative element, within the cities, where the public can feel the essence of solidity, electricity and communication.

Christmas Star is not a project to build another community that is concerned with its own comforts and needs, secure within its own compound, but a project that requires people to concatenate, endure and create a cathexis in unity, willing to exhaust themselves to hold to the timeframe of the apocalypse without separating themselves from the future Golden Age. Any community of the near future that will survive the whirlpool of man's atrocities must recognize that there is a mission and that "this mission requires the design of a whole metaphysical position free of limiting heresies. It requires strong and competent leadership in moments of freedom. It requires action in terms of individual immortality and collective evolution. It requires sacrifice if and only if a step on the path to God is possible."

"In the past we did not read the signs, heed the warnings, respect or nurture our planet. We arrogantly separated humanity from nature and from God. The apocalypse is not a symbol of natural ignorance. It is a symbol of blind stupidity. War is constant, death and starvation are universal. The horrors of torture and genocide steadily increase. Humanity is losing itself. The lack of qualified spiritual healers and diviners is evident in the rise of suicide in all of its forms. Are we willing to endure the rigors of change?"

The warrior priests must come forward out of the mist of mysticism. "The essence of mysticism is connection." An essential aspect of this connection is that of the Earth and the

sacred plan needing to link them together with those souls willing to apply pressure to learn and implement natural, healthy technologies and earthly rituals to regain a balance that emits a beacon to civilization for the long, awaited time of great rejoicing on our planet and also in need of the exigent situation to awaken this deep inner commitment.

Some of the healthy technologies planned are various solar and wind-operated utilities, greenhouses, underground life support systems and home environs, learning centers, emergency storage and communication facilities and continued healing environmental landscaping. There are occasional workshops and celebrations incorporating traditional sweats, music, speakers, feasting and healing circles.

Visiting is open to serious people and families looking to share and communicate information and experiences and able to provide their own material support. Christmas Star is being built to fashion ways that will change civilization. If you are looking for an environment already set up to provide your needs or a location that will deny your responsibilities to the world, or if archery and firearms training, basic first aid practice, intense survival information, a congenial relationship with local ranchers and law enforcement officers represent negative connotations, then the painstakingly slow sieve and distilling process will show you that this is not a place for you to make the genuine conversion from self to humanity and God. No one can face this path alone. Write or call anytime.

Writing by John Cohen and excerpts from Chris Moore from the Blue Flame Atlantis Mystery School Training (marked by quotations).

CIRCLE PINES CENTER

Cooperative Summer Camp with a Focus on Peace Education

**Circle Pines Center
8650 Mullen Road
Delton, MI 49046
(616) 623-5555**

Circle Pines Center, a non-profit educational and recreational cooperative, offers an outstanding summer camp program for children, adults and families. Since 1938, Circle Pines has served as an inter-racial and inter-generational common ground which attracts people from throughout the Midwest for conferences, recreation, camping, healing and group learning experiences. The Center is located north of Kalamazoo on 360 acres of rolling meadows, pine and hardwood forests and a beautiful spring-fed lake.

Our work with peace education is based on the premise of the caring relationships we develop and model with each other will further efforts down the line in supporting each other in group actions. Circle Pines has the advantage of its contacts with people in urban areas who can be a resource for the camp program--which consciously addresses larger social issues.

Circle Pines' programs are a powerful kind of "peace education" for campers who live in a cooperative setting that values individual participation within the community. Campers become the life of the community, sharing in the tasks that are necessary for a group of individuals to live together. Morning work projects, at which each camper helps as is appropriate to his or her age, involve whole foods cooking, harvesting vegetables from the large organic garden, construction projects such as painting an outhouse or repairing a cabin, developing nature trails and cleaning of community facilities.

This focus on peace education is furthered by recognizing that personal differences often arise when people come together to work and play. We learn to settle these disagreements non-violently through a variety of conflict resolution techniques. There is an emphasis on group problem-solving that recognizes the importance of listening for others' feelings and expression. In addition, many traditional and new games are non-competitive, such as cooperative volley ball, in which participants rotate under the net; in this way, the teams' members are constantly changing so the objective of the game becomes to play your best with your friends as opposed to playing against and beating the other team.

Afternoons provide opportunities to learn creative skills in drama, arts and crafts, photography, nature and earth science studies, music, group recreation, canoeing and water safety. A dramatic performance with dance and music that relates to peace issues is developed by the campers during each of the two-week sessions. Special adventures such as rock-climbing, river canoe trips, challenging a ropes and obstacle course, blueberry picking, visiting a dairy farm or bird sanctuary and overnight hikes offer campers further ways of learning and growing in a rural environment through group activities.

Some evenings are spent building unit solidarity by playing new games, preparing skits, making popcorn, telling stories and singing around the campfire. Other evenings bring the entire Circle Pines community together for cooperative games, folk dance and instruction, dramatic productions, sharing talents with one another or participating in the customs of other cultures.

The Children's Summer Camp program runs from July 7 to August 17; three, two-week sessions are available for ages 8 to 15, who sign up for one of three units based on age.

Three Young Adult programs are designed to encourage young people to become self-reliant, responsible leaders of the community. Youth Work Camp, for ages 15 - 18, offers a six-week work and adventure program to develop stamina, build group awareness, gain new skills and cope with strenuous outdoor living. After working on a special construction project at Circle Pines, the campers venture out on a challenging trip to the Lake Superior wilderness area, led by expert counselors.

The Counselors- and Staff-in-Training program for 16 - 18 year olds involves 7 1/2 weeks of working with the camp staff in orientation and the children's camp as well as doing special unit activities. Youth Institute, at the end of camp, is a week long experiment in cooperative democracy for 13 - 18 year olds. The Youth explore a theme of their choosing such as "The Arts in Society" through workshops and discussions and they enjoy the beach, creative arts and prepare their own meals as a community.

For families who wish to experience Circle Pines as a family with other families, we offer two week-long Family Camps (June and August). The first family camp is especially designed for families with young children, while the second is for families of all ages.

Adults and under camp-age children are welcome anytime. Visitors often contribute to the camp program by sharing their skills, telling a story or participating in camp activities.

THE COMMUNITY

Melanie and Michael Rios
414 N. Edgewood Street
Arlington, VA 22201
(707) 528-3204

The Community is an intentional family, a neighborhood, a network of friends, and a way of living. A dozen or so folks live here, ranging in age from 8 months to 71 years. Many of us have lived together for a decade or more. Our goal is to be a loving family and good neighbors in whatever way we can.

We have several houses on a city/suburban block, though many people in our network live elsewhere as well. We see community as an attitude and a lifestyle rather than a particular set of buildings; loving communication is the glue that holds us together. There are no membership lists; people establish the connections that they feel are best for themselves.

We tend to be individualists, living with few formal structures. Over the last ten years, there have often been more businesses than members! Our current businesses include a chain of computer stores, a drug education program, property management, and commercial art. Our network includes artists, carpenters, musicians, teachers, healers, inventors, entertainers, writers, and "guerrilla capitalists."

We share a strong sense of spirituality, without endorsing any particular guru, dogma, or religion. Our lifestyle centers on everyday living, with a little extra consciousness and concern about the world around us.

Our three pre-school children are the focus of much of our daily recreations and joy. We especially welcome other parents who want mutual support in the child-raising process, sharing child care, chores, and play. We are also considering home schooling in the future.

Other special joys are acoustical music and group singing, bicycling, hiking, conversing, eating healthful foods, and laughing. (We try to avoid drugs, quarrels, and artificial flavoring.)

We intend to be lifelong friends and family, living together as best we can. We seek new members in a rather relaxed way; we are open to extending our family circle, but don't feel compelled to do so. Visitors are welcome, and are expected to share in our work as well as play.

If you would like to visit, please contact us at least a week in advance. You may arrive by car or public transportation--we live a short metro ride and walk from downtown Washington, D.C., in an area with lots of green space and towering oak trees. Please do not bring alcohol, tobacco, or other drugs. Give us a call if you'd like more information.

COMPTCHE COMMUNITY FARMS, INC.

P. O. Box 5258
Santa Rosa, CA 95402-5258

Comptche Community Farms, Inc. was formed for the purpose of establishing a rural, residential community with two major aims: to create a loving and supportive living environment for ourselves and our children in which we can grow and learn freely together; and to foster the art of living close to the land, serving as conscious, respectful stewards of the natural world around us, and directly experiencing the bonds which connect us to the earth and all its various forms of life. We see these aims as necessarily intertwined, each enhancing the other, and both together expressing our best vision of a responsible and joyful way of life.

We are first and foremost a family community. Our main focus is aimed at providing a healthy and wholesome shared community environment for ourselves and our children in a rural farm setting.

A Short History of CCF:

Russ & Jane and Lynn & Michael were the moving force behind the original purchase of our 102-acre parcel in May 1983. Our property is nestled in a beautiful mountain valley several miles outside of the tiny town of Comptche, in Mendocino County, California. The valley is about 12 miles inland from the Northern California coastal town of Mendocino. From the Golden Gate Bridge in San Francisco, its about a 3-hour drive North.

The land itself is breathtakingly beautiful. Some say it is the most beautiful they've seen anywhere in the area. The weather is cooler than the Ukiah valley to the East, but well out of the coastal fog zone. Temperatures range from 50's to 90's in summer and from 20's to 50's in winter. The land itself was used for many years as a farm. More than a third

of the land is flat enough for cultivation, with excellent soil, and has ample water year round from two creeks and several springs. We are, in fact, at the head waters of the Navarro River, and are very fortunate in having plenty of water resources available.

Since the original purchase of the bare land in 1983 by Russ and Jane, a number of improvements have been made:

- roads have been put in;

- an irrigation-quality water system has been established which includes a 4600-gallon storage tank, with 7,200 feet of 1.5" PVC pipe and a solar-powered pumping system;

- a 25-line phone cable has been laid throughout the property;

- a small cabin has been built and added onto for use by members and guests;

- a 50-tree orchard has been planted and drip irrigation system has been installed for trees and garden areas;

- a fenced berry patch has been developed and planted in raspberries and blackberries;

- a 2000 sq. ft. vegetable garden space has been fenced and planted and is now producing for our personal use;

- an area has been leveled for an eventual greenhouse planned to be 120 ft. x 40 ft.;

- several potential building sites have been bulldozed or cleared.

Until about September 1986, Russ and Jane (with some financial help from Lynn and Michael) were pretty much going it alone, while looking for others to join them in building a community. They were also handling the entire mortgage by

themselves, which was an enormous burden for a single family.

Then in October 1986 Glen & Zarifah joined, and we all decided to reorganize. Since that time all mortgage payments, taxes and other development costs have been shared equally among the families. As part of that reorganization, in Jan. '87 we incorporated as a California stock corporation. This was a big step toward consolidating and defining the legal and financial commitment of our community. In September 1987 the legal title to the land and tools was formally transferred by Russ & Jane into the name of the corporation, "Comptche Community Farms, Inc." Each of us is now a legally equal voting shareholder in the corporation. All decisions are made by meetings of the members (us), so far entirely by consensus. The land itself and assets of the community are owned in common through the corporation, not by individuals. Our operating rules are all set out in a "Shareholders' Agreement" which serves as a contract among us as a community of people with common goals and the intention to live and work closely together.

Plans for the Future:

Our initial goal is to all congregate in the Santa Rosa area to be close to one another and the land for work and play projects. Our orchard, garden and other activities will require more of our time and labor as we develop our community, and right now we caretake the property on a rotating basis between the two families in the area, using the existing cabin for that purpose. As yet none of us can live on the land full time.

The land payments, though steep, are not so fierce when split among several families. But they are a monthly financial responsibility we must meet as a group. As additional families join us, payments will be split more ways and be less of a burden individually. Furthermore, they are fixed payments, and in less than 7 years the land will be paid off! From that point on all of our funds can go into improvements and buildings on the land.

What to do if you are interested in learning more:

This should give you a pretty good idea of how we are organized and what membership responsibilities are. Naturally we've had to simplify or leave out a lot of the details, which are written out in our Shareholders' Agreement and other legal documents. If you are serious about the possibility of joining us, we will be happy to provide you with copies of our written agreements among ourselves in which all the nitty-gritty details are precisely spelled out.

We are now looking for at least two other families with a commitment to creating a supportive and cooperative lifestyle in a shared rural farm community, and who are also financially responsible and capable of fulfilling our financial requirements.

If you are still seriously interested please write us, send a picture or give us a call to tell us about yourselves. In Northern California you can reach Russ and Jane at (707) 546-3809 or Glen & Zarifah at (707) 838-3772, and in Southern California you can call Lynn & Michael at (213) 450-6908. The next step would be to plan with us a time when you could come to the area to meet and talk with each of us personally.

SEEKING PARTNERS...

Russ and Jane Neuman
12154 Occidental Rd.
Sebastopol, CA 95472
(707) 874-2918

Two families with young children have 102 acres of beautiful land in Comptche (15 miles east of Mendocino, CA). Springs, creeks, good farm soil. Wish to establish a land cooperative of perhaps six to eight families who share a desire to live more simply in a rural area and build their own home. Gardens, tools, land expenses shared as a group. We seek new members who are able to assist with land payments and who have skills appropriate to our community vision.

Robert and Dianne McCormick
HC 61, Box 350
Boswell, OK 74727

Community located on 120 acres of pine forested land in a county of 10,000 in southeastern Oklahoma. Looking for new members who seek an unpolluted haven offering a chance to work with likeminded people for political and environmental change on a local level for the creation of an environment conducive to intellectual growth. No age preferences, but prospective new members should be financially independent or have mobile careers. Community is not yet entirely self-sufficient. Community is based on privacy and individual ownership of dwellings and household goods with flexible interaction between families/individuals. Cash buy-in required for homesite.

EMISSARY FOUNDATION INTERNATIONAL

**Box 9, 100 Mile House
B.C., Canada, VOK 2E0**

A Zulu tribal chieftain, an airline stewardess, an Italian princess, and a solar energy consultant: What do all these individuals have in common? All are friends, dedicated to expressing their innate potential, and all are associated with the Emissary Foundation International.

This nonprofit organization, among other activities, operates several communities and communal homes around the world. The facilities haven't been established to save money, grow organic gardens, or pioneer complementary healing techniques, though there is developed expertise in these areas. Our sense of community is based upon our love and respect for life and its inherent design. We offer spiritual leadership courses, assist any who wish to reveal more of their potential, and celebrate the myriad ways in which the awakening consciousness of mankind is currently being made evident.

Our association began in 1932, when Lloyd Meeker, the son of a midwestern farmer and minister, discovered--in the course of searching for his purpose--a 'spiritual' identity. In 1940, he met Lord Martin Cecil who, not long before, had left his family's ancestral home in England to travel the wilderness of British Columbia. These men immediately found a shared sense of commission and, as they continued living with vision and integrity, many chose to associate with them.

Today, Emissaries reside in some 200 centers, including communal facilities, from New York to California and from England to South Africa, but many who speak of themselves as Emissaries live in suburban homes and work in cities and on farms. Rather than spotlighting any

one of our 12 larger communities, I believe it would be more useful to attempt to convey some essences of our experience as a body of friends and, secondarily, as an organization spanning six continents.

Each center is a unique combination of factors and reflects the individuals who compose it. In some communities, several residents are employed locally and pay room and board, or cover such costs as are required: the mortgage, house maintenance, food, etc....some operate businesses, from medical offices to farms and janitorial services...and others, occupied with running homes and raising children, are supported by those generating income.

Communal living was proven useful in bringing together people with diverse personalities and backgrounds, since it requires each individual to interact in a deep and genuine way in order for blending to occur. For example, I correspond with and visit intentional communities throughout the world. However, before departing for, say, Denmark or Louisiana, I have to take into account the necessities of my home, where 125 people reside. Will there be a sufficient number on hand to take care of the canning and juicing at harvest time? Perhaps I need to take a paying position locally and bring home an income for a period of time. Perhaps I don't need to travel at all. Each one is required to be aware of his or her own sphere of activity within a larger context, since our worlds are larger than our tiny communities.

We find nuclear family life is an important aspect within the context of our larger community, and a powerful means of focusing creative living.

Our children are most often educated in the public school system. This is a mixed blessing, but it has appeared valuable thus far, for them to be exposed to "everyday" society. We find that the rich quality of our lifestyle remains the dominant factor in our young ones' lives.

Central to our collective function is our respect for coordination. We each freely offer our unique views to those in coordinating positions, permitting an overall perspective to be brought into focus. We recognize that alone one person doesn't see all the factors in any given situation, and that an elevated perspective is essential. Functioning together in this shared process of creative living is a far cry from the self-serving attitudes so prevalent in our world.

We are also active beyond the immediate scope of our intentional community. Professionals in various fields offer lectures, workshops or produce a selection of publications. *Business Dynamics*, for example, a newsletter published by our 100 Mile House business group, receives contributions from around the world. The Whole Health Institute, an association of healing practitioners, presents workshops worldwide and publishes *Healing Currents*. Media professionals find the Association for Responsible Communication (ARC) and its newsletter *In Touch* useful in

bringing a broad sense of responsibility into a profession often preoccupied with sales and sensationalism. A wilderness training program, "Educo", offers one and two-week rigorous experiences of self-discovery to the adventurous of all ages. Here, at 100 Mile House, we publish *Integrity International,* a quarterly magazine which circulates in nearly 60 countries.

Among the events Emissaries sponsored or participated in, in recent years, were The Fourth World Wilderness Congress in Colorado which brought more than 1,000 people together to consider the critical state of the environment and to see what could be done about it. Among those present were James Baker, U.S. Secretary of the Treasury, Gro Harlem Brundtland, Prime Minister of Norway and Chairman of the World Commission on the Environment. China's Minister of Forestry, and David Rockefeller, international banker and financier. The Entertainment Summit, a precedent-setting gathering of some of the United States' and Soviet Union's most influential film directors, screen writers, actors and journalists designed to "examine the damaging, often vicious stereotypes each country has reinforced in movies and television and to move beyond the myth of "the enemy". In 1989, ARC will be jointly sponsoring a significant media event with *The Christian Science Monitor,* entitled "Communication as Service: Media's Role in Shaping the World", and The Stewardship Community will be hosting a conference designed to examine the state of the global environment and our responsibility for its wise stewardship.

We believe that a new world is appearing, while the old one is creaking at its seams. The world, we are discovering, is but an extension of our consciousness. As we alter our outlook, a national border may disappear, a battle may cease, or--more immediately--a new friend may be discovered. There are increasing numbers of individuals and organizations learning that beyond paths, disciplines, and techniques, there's and implicit design to life that works. Our wish is to align with this design in an increasingly intelligent and balanced way.

by Dave Thatcher

Reprinted (in part) with Permission from The Mother Earth News, © copyright, The Mother Earth News, Inc., Hendersonville, NC 28791. All Rights Reserved.

AN INVITATION TO RESPOND

You are invited to contemplate the idea below, to sincerely share your ideas about a just and peaceful world:

Clearly life on the planet is in jeopardy. What will it take to reverse the fear, the weapons, the pollution, the monopoly, the intervention...; and project life toward abundance, cooperation and environmental and social compassion? How can we experience such a miracle? "Consciousness creates form" (Seth). Please be practical. (Less than 500 words.) Are you willing to be published?   yes ❑ no❑. Please include your name, address, and a short description of yourself.

It is our intention to circulate the contributions, to create a continuum and an on-going forum. Facts, feelings, ideas, positive creations are welcomed. Transformation is inevitable. It is clearly the will of the human race to live on abundantly well into the future.

Send your responses to:

NAMASTE CONSCIOUSNESS
Box 578
Center Barnstead, NH 03225

P. S. Feel free to copy and distribute.

THE FARM

**The Farm
Summertown, TN 38483
by Barbara Elliott**

The farm is a unique and ever-changing community. It was established in 1971 as a spiritual collective on 1,000 acres of land in southern middle Tennessee. It grew to 1,750 acres and 1,500 people at the peak of its population. The Farm's acreage today is still the same, but the population has dropped to around 300. Many wonder why and what were the changes leading to this.

To provide food, housing, clothing, medical and dental care for 1,500 people was no easy task and financing these operations was always a scramble. A small, but loyal, group of carpenters along with other individuals and crews earned money in the neighboring area which went into the common treasury. However, the number of people to be supported always far outnumbered those supporting them and the ends did not come close to meeting, even with the addition of many individuals' inheritances. Quite a bit of debt was incurred just to meet ordinary living expenses and community functions. That, plus a failed farming venture and a couple of major medical bills, left an indebted Farm and exhausted credit sources to the new Board of Directors, elected in 1983, whose job it was to somehow fix it all up and make it better! By that time, quite a few members had become discouraged with their limited resources and standards of living and left, seeking more prosperous living conditions. The Board of Directors had little recourse and made the bold move of changing the economic system on the Farm. They gave a few months notice that soon everyone would be responsible for their family's income as well as to pay the Foundation a sum every week for each adult living on the Farm. This weekly sum would enable us to continue to pay on the collective debt and to keep the gate and other community functions operating.

Through all of these changes, we've managed to keep our school, clinic, midwives, bakery, soy dairy, store, and several other small businesses operating. In some ways it has not been an easy transition. The economic reality of southern middle Tennessee quickly became apparent -- high unemployment and generally low wages were important considerations for many folks leaving. There are close to 200 former Farm members now living in the Nashville area and there are several other pockets around the country where former Farm members have congregated and feel close ties with each other. Sorting out the legalities and logistics of this complicated and unusual experiment has been extremely challenging for all of the members of the Farm's Board of Directors, and even after years of hard work, there's still a lot to be decided for them and the whole community.

Those of us still here are glad to live out in the country with like-minded friends in a relatively safe, open, and free environment. The swimming hole offers relief from the summer heat and the winters are usually mild. We are interested in having new members. Some of us partially and others totally support themselves with jobs within the community, and others have jobs in nearby towns. There is work in the area and opportunity to start small businesses if effort is made. In the last few years, we've installed the previously long-awaited water, electric and telephone lines and there are plenty of building sites. It is a great environment for kids to grow up in. Any individuals or families who are interested in joining the community would need to make a financial investment towards housing as well as bring along some means of income, or find employment in the area. If you are interested in receiving more information about visiting and/or joining the community, send $3 to: Information at the above address, specifying what information you're interested in.

THE FOUNDATION FOR FEEDBACK LEARNING

A Non-profit, Tax-exempt, Non-religious, Educational Research Organization

135 Corson Ave.
Staten Island, NY 10301
(718) 720-5378

Proposal for the Formation of a Communities Center--a Central Office to Serve the Work of Communities of All Kinds, Everywhere

The world-wide development of cooperative communities is impressive and important. I don't think it necessary to belabor the need for alternative forms of economic, political, social organization. Almost everybody who has thought about it agrees that what we have doesn't work very well.

Perhaps it will require the evolvement of the world's first successful model of direct democracy, to produce a safe, sane setting for satisfying human life in harmony with the environment. By direct democracy I mean the full informed participation of all of the governed in the governing process.

It is reasonable to assume that if a good model of direct democracy will ever have a chance to succeed at all, it will take the efforts of many small experimental units, and many individuals deeply committed to their own growth in the process.

Until now, it has been difficult for most small intentional communities to do well economically, while trying to maintain a degree of independence from the influence and the pressures of the larger society to whom they eventually hope to bring meaningful change. Unfortunately a good deal of their development up to this point has happened largely in isolation and under serious economic stress. In the result, too often, experimentation with alternative forms of social, political organization, and even personal development, have been neglected in favor of

trying to meet bottom-line survival needs. Indeed the bulk of these experimental communities simply have not survived.

Perhaps part of the solution is good networking, which is indeed evolving in many forms in a number of places. What seems to be necessary is on-site coordination of all of these efforts. Everyone is familiar with the advantage of pooling resources within communities. I think it is time we began to think of putting our pooling capabilities into practice between communities, in as broad a perspective as possible. We need to find ways to share resources of all kinds. Together we can develop many things not readily affordable to most of us alone. Perhaps sharing experience, ideas, even dreams is as necessary as pooling expertise and material resources.

The dilemma is--how to do this, how to achieve good coordination between communities without loss of the autonomy that each group must have to ensure its own development.

The Foundation for Feedback Learning, a small New York based intentional community, is proposing the establishment of a Center in the city that will serve as a clearing house for the materials and possibly the products of communities of all kinds, all over the world. Such a center might serve the need of many communities for economic, political, social, informational, technological and organizational support. We have a lot to give each other and a lot to take from each other. We need a place in which this exchange can conveniently occur.

New York City seems a good place for this to happen because most people come through it one time or another, and so could readily avail themselves of the services the Cen-

ter could offer. If they work, possibly Center's offices could eventually also be located on the West Coast, probably in San Francisco, and in the center of the country, perhaps in Chicago. In time such Center's offices might be available in capitals all over the world. Ideally these Centers would be located on university campuses and their work would be supplemented by the academic community and its many resources.

What we hope for is the development of a vehicle that has no philosophy of its own and as far as possible, no decision making authority of any kind. It should consist of offices; meeting rooms; workshop space; possibly display space for communities' products, a good book, periodical, audio and video-tape and film library; and as talented a staff as can be found. It should provide opportunity for whatever any group of communities want to do and can afford. What we are proposing is an office and a good staff available for whatever is wanted. It seems possible that such a neutral networking agency could conceivably provide the connections that can bring a world-wide community movement together into a very viable force for whatever it, or any part of it, wants to accomplish.

However, many of the people we spoke with agree with us, that all this will have value only in propor-

tion to its ability to provide such a unifying, resource-sharing capability, without ANY loss of autonomy, for any community. Even more importantly, it will be necessary to avoid any attempt to eliminate the differences between communities. We are suggesting that much of the strength of the movement will come because of, rather than in spite of, their differences. Hopefully, what will emerge will be a loose conduit that flows between unlike, small, alternatives for autonomous, but coordinated political units, in which many diverse individuals can meet their personal needs while making their optimal social contribution.

The purpose of such a neutral structure would be to make it possible to approach the media, the markets, the universities, or political units in the name of whatever an individual or group of individual communities want to achieve with such an approach to the media, the markets, or whatever--serving them an only them--and only by their agreement.

The Center's office would make opportunities and options available. It would outline the costs and the probable risks and gains. It would distribute such information to all communities. When responses are received, these would again be combined, summarized and distributed for further comments. The Center's office would probably conduct periodic polls among communities about issues of concern to them. But they would make no decisions and take no action except at the request of the specific communities to be served by that action.

Therefore, from our point of view, it is most important that the Center's office not itself be a community. If a number of communities want to have a selling office out of the Center, then they will make their arrangements for that as an individual cluster of communities for whom the Center will sell. If they

want to share know-how, labor, talent, money, or whatever, the Center's office would merely help them do it. The Center's guidelines, advertising, and procedures would all be approved by the communities served by the specific activity involved before they are undertaken. If the staff of the Center chooses to live together as a community, that might be fine, provided that that community has no activity other than conducting the business of the Center's office. Again, that business of the Center's office will be determined by the communities it specifically serves, and only them--never by the staff of the Center itself.

This kind of neutrality is assuredly a tricky business. It would probably require that the Center's office not even have a fixed Board of Directors, but only those communities affected by an action would be authorized to shape and determine the nature of that specific action. The obvious reason for this suggestion that the autonomy of the communities be so meticulously safeguarded, is the assumption that it is in the differences between communities, and the autonomy for each needed to sustain such difference, that the strength of the "communities movement" might emerge. This idea received substantial support from many sources at the convention in Edinburgh in the summer of 1988.

Aiming at coordination without control is ambitious, but possibly necessary. I don't think, nor do I believe most of us think, that any of us have found substantial answers to society's problems. We certainly haven't found very viable solutions to the problem of hostility between people or to the breakdown of communication and problem-solving machinery that plagues us all. Perhaps it is in the possibility of pooling resources while maintaining differences that a new kind of unity and new kind of strength can be found. The resources of the Center's office we're proposing would be offered to

all but violent communities. Perhaps our prohibition against the use of coercive force is all the guidelines, or even all the agreement we'll ever need. We envision clusters of communities forming to achieve some purposes and dissolving to re-form in other clusters for other purposes. This fluidity in itself may provide the form needed to unify our forces enough to give us strength without pressing us into a mold in which we create new dogma faster than we break out of the old ones.

The proposed "communities center" could offer many needed services to individual communities, their members, and those interested in helping the community movement.

1. It could be a central information distribution center. Friends of community, or people looking for a community to join, or people who are just curious, could come to the "Communities Center" and get the latest information about any or all communities.

2. Ongoing workshops on "community", its purposes and problems, successes and failures, could also be made available through such a "Communities Center".

3. A "Communities Center" might also act as a clearing house for a speakers' bureau, film and/or slide showing or rentals, and for all of our many individual and collective special events.

4. A travel service kind of arrangement might be made that would allow people to plan trips all over the country--in fact all over the world, staying at communities for a weekend, or week, for some months, or perhaps just for dinner, all along their route.

5. An important networking function could be served by the "Communities Center", by establishing a mailing service that makes it possible to send any piece of literature to all communities--and to get literature from whatever community you are interested in.

6. A work clearing house might serve a very valuable function.

7. Perhaps the joint fundraising possibilities offered by a "Communities Center" might be among its most valuable contributions.

8. The most important contribution of such a Center is its potential for publicity and for the feedback that it might generate.

Staffing for the "Communities Center" would have to be a gradual process. It could be started with one full time person would would begin with a "friends of community" recruiting effort that might provide volunteers, fundraisers, etc.

We at the Foundation for Feedback Learning would be prepared to house, feed and pay minimal expenses for such a director of the Center.

Rents in New York City are high. Ideally, housing might eventually be on the campus of one of New York's academic institutions.

If you are interested in helping to get a "Community Center's Office" started in New York City, write or call the above.

FRIENDS OF THE RETARDED, INC.

205 Bosley Avenue
Towson, MD 21204
(301) 296-2454

Our organization, Friends of the Retarded, has worked diligently for many years to establish an intentional community in the state of Maryland. We are looking for people who have either lived in an intentional farming community and/or have interest in establishing and working in such a community with mentally retarded adults.

Presently, we have a lease for a 120-plus acre farm that includes two houses, a barn, cropland, pasture and woodlands. We have also raised a considerable amount of money for renovations, operating expenses, etc.

Although the community would have to follow certain Maryland state regulations governing programs for the mentally retarded, the nature of the community could take whatever form the members of the community wanted. Further,

the community will be self-governing with our organization acting as a supportive and fund-raising entity.

What we would like to do is establish the community first and then integrate our mentally retarded citizens into the community as long as they can be easily absorbed.

We have long recognized that society at large has failed to deal adequately with people and their problems. In an intentional community, it seems to us, people become educated in a cooperative way of life, with new attitudes and values, in an environment that enhances personal growth. Further, people learn to live as an inter-related part of a whole, balancing the needs of others with their own. If this environment is beneficial to most people, how much more beneficial is such an environment to our mentally retarded citizens where they have the opportunity to live and work with loving, supportive friends? Whereas society at large is difficult for most of us to cope with, for a mentally retarded person

coping is much more difficult and often overwhelming.

It is our belief that an intentional community can offer all its members a safe, supportive and loving environment of friends where people can grow and contribute to the success of the community. Can you imagine what this would mean to a mentally retarded person?

We see all kinds of possibilities: crop farming/gardening, horticulture, developing an orchard, a bakery, livestock, a dairy, food processing, crafts, etc. depending on the interests and abilities of the members of the community.

If this sounds like something that you might consider, drop me a line. I will contact you right away for further discussion. It would be helpful if you include something about yourself. Children are welcome.

Yours for a Better Life
for the Retarded,

Dr. Lee Goren, President

FUTURES

A Parable of Five Christians

111 Bolink
Berea, KY 40403

Jim is a Christian. He has lived every year of this century. Now he is a very comfortable landlord and moneylender according to the customs of society. Rent pricks his conscience because it impoverishes the poor. Interest pricks his conscience because it impoverishes the poor. Jim sincerely wants to invest in liberation rather than subjugation of other people. In order to be a 100% Christian he must recast the system.

Marcia is a Christian. She enjoys growing food, she is an organic gardener. Her way to prevent bugs and blight is to enrich the soil. Marcia feels deeply for all the people who pollute their bodies with snacks and fast foods and sweets but her compassion is repressed by dietary customs of the American Way. Marcia knows by experience that "You are what you eat." She wants a system that is geared to wellness, not sickness. She can't recast the system alone.

Gus builds solarhouses that are affordable, comfortable and beautiful. He wants kids to have a chance; no slums. Gus wants to apply his Christian expertise to emancipation of poor people, but the system is built on profit, not on service. He dreams about cutting housing costs one half. Christians should cooperate, build their own, live where they work, move some utilities into their community hall. Gear up with Marcia's food crew.

Susan is not sure that she is a Christian, but she acts like one. She does not want to nurse strangers with whom she has no identity. Rather, she desires to nurse friends, companions, neighbors, in a 100% Christian colony. She prefers womb-to-tomb wholistic nursing. Wellness includes family planning, midwifery, baby clinic, first aid, disease prevention, senior care and dying. Susan is willing to help recast the system.

Grace is a gracious, loving teacher. Her Christian witness is compulsive. She thinks people can enliven and enlighten themselves in intimate groups. Montessori way for tots. Consensus way for adolescents. As for adults, "None of us is as smart as all of us." A community can be sort of a folk school from cradle to the grave. Christians share each other, hold things in common, are of one spirit and love transcends need. Compare Acts 4:31-37.

Then a miracle, these five families found each other and formed a larger family which recast the system from competition to cooperation. Jim loaned without interest for the farm. All transferred equity from individual to mutual living units. The food crew recast the farm system - perennials in place of annuals, compost in place of chemicals, fish in place of beef. Housing has solar in place of fossil. And the noon gatherings for food, worship, service and fun bond them all together with consensus in place of conflict.

Christians, with hands and feet, recast the system. Workers without war because allowance is below IRS. NO poverty--street people with character get lifetime jobs and dignity. Christian singles are sustained by affection in place of stress. Seniors on custodial care in soul fraternity. No AIDS because eros is gratified by God's design. This parable is based on a mountain, not in a skyscraper.

The Lord is my Pace-setter, I shall not rush; He makes me stop and rest for quiet intervals. He provides me with images of stillness, which restore my serenity; He leads me in the ways of efficiency through calmness of mind, and his guidance is peace. Even though I have a great many things to accomplish each day, I will not fret, for His presence is here. His timelessness, His all importance, will keep me in balance. He prepares refreshment and renewal in the midst of my activity, by anointing my mind with His oils of tranquility. My cup of joyous energy overflows. Surely harmony and effectiveness shall be the fruits of my hours, for I shall walk in the pace of my Lord, and dwell in His house forever.
--Spiritual Frontiers--a Japanese version of the 23rd Psalm.

HARBIN HOT SPRINGS

P.O. Box 782
Middletown, CA 95461
(707) 987-2477 or
(800) 622-2477 (CA only)

Harbin Hot Springs is a vibrant community of 135 persons (125 adults, 10 children) who have come together to create and manifest the dreams of the New Age. Our 1,160 acres of woods, meadows and streams are nestled in the valley of majestic Mount Harbin and located two hours north of the San Francisco Bay Area. Our community shares this beautiful environment with visitors, both individuals and groups. We operate, maintain and improve the facilities of our resort, retreat and teaching center.

Harbin Hot Springs is a healing place, where the sacred land and the waters work to restore people's physical and spiritual energy. In our competitive western society, people need places such as Harbin to show them that humankind is meant to work out its problems together--that we are not separate, but part of the whole. Indeed, if we are to survive as a planet, we may have to learn this lesson on oneness--that our every action has an impact on the entire universe. Rather than compete with one another, we learn not just to tolerate, but to celebrate our differences and the rich diversity of our lifestyles.

For centuries, Native Americans believed Harbin Hot Springs had magical healing properties. In the nineteenth and early twentieth centuries, the property functioned as a European-type spa. After a colorful history and gradual decline, the resort closed down in 1968. In 1972, the property was purchased by one of our community's founding members. Several years later a group of residents, including the individual owner, met together to discuss and decide what they wanted the com-munity to be, and were surprised at the extent to which they agreed. That agreement became the principles of Heart Consciousness Church. Heart Consciousness Church, Inc., a non-profit corporation was formed in 1975, and the ownership of Harbin Hot Springs was transferred to it. Besides providing a conceptual framework for the community, the church serves as an umbrella organization under which many activities can develop.

The transformation since those beginnings has been remarkable. Renovation and new construction has been taking place at an impressive rate.

The School of Shiatsu and Massage holds classes and certification intensives that are developed and taught by several of the community's residents.

Our main income is derived from operating the hot springs resort and from renting space to outside conference and workshop groups. The four conference centers we've constructed or renovated can accommodate groups ranging from 14 to 300 people.

Aside from construction, members work mostly at jobs connected with visitors or with community administration such as office reception, bookkeeping, housekeeping, landscaping, security, massage, computer services, publications and special projects. Some of us have our own businesses, and a few have outside jobs. Our community includes therapists, school teachers, musicians, artists, contractors, cooks, laborers, skilled tradespeople, writers and computer professionals, to identify a few. Many of us came here with the specific intention of lending our energies permanently to creating a better life situation, while others simply wanted to stay a while to learn new skills or to take time out in our lives for reassessment while relaxing in the natural hot pools. Often, the second kind of motivation has transformed into the first.

People newly arriving at Harbin Springs are in a three-month training program and are called Cadre. They learn work skills, doing work training on a five-day-a-week basis. They attend two nightly meetings a week to study the process of living in a community and receive training in our beliefs and how the community works. Cadre are not paid. They live in dormitory-class spaces and receive a weekly credit for food. A person graduates from Cadre when they do two things: first, show work skill by finding a regular work assignment in the community or by proving that they do not need community work to survive, and; second to demonstrate harmonious behavior and understanding of the principles of the Church and community.

Most of us work 25 to 40 hours a week here, but usually in a much more relaxed atmosphere than that of our counterparts in the business world. Cottage industries are encouraged and sometimes assisted.

A deposit of $250 is required of all residents-applicants upon arrival at Harbin Hot Springs. This will be refunded, less any charges due, should the person leave the community.

In addition, there are some initial membership dues which may either be paid in full upon arrival, or paid gradually.

Use of drugs is forbidden at Harbin Hot Springs to preserve the sacred nature of the land. We are a non-smoking, clothing-optional community. Use of tobacco is prohibited on Harbin Hot Springs property.

Our current policy regarding pets is that none are permitted.

Decisions at Harbin Hot Springs are made by committees. Resident members are encouraged to take as much responsibility as they wish within the community--anyone who joins the community can participate in its governmental structure by demonstrating commitment, competence and willingness to take on responsibility.

Although Harbin has a definite structure and operational base, its lifeblood for new activities is new people and the ability to incorporate new ideas into the existing framework. We have an open-door policy--anyone who is sincerely willing to contribute to the community is welcome. We have no required beliefs or practices. Our resident members are people who, in their own ways, feel a resonance with the New Age ideals of the human potential movement, the holistic, natural movement and universal spirituality. There is an acceptance and openness to different ideas, beliefs, and spiritual paths.

While you may just drop in, there are many important details concerning visiting, meals, workshops, work exchange and residency that are not described here, so we do recommend calling or writing before visiting us.

HEARTLIGHT CENTER

67138 Shimmel Road
Sturgis, MI 49091
(616) 651-2234

We greet you in love. Our hearts have called us to share with you a joyful opportunity: Heartlight Center.

We know that deep within the heart of all mankind is a longing to live as brothers and sisters in love, joy and peace, not in some distant place or time, but here and now.

Heartlight Center is offering opportunities through its programs for you to become involved so that, along with others, you may begin to know your true self and your purpose in life.

What is Heartlight Center? It is a place where people are striving to live the Kingdom of God 24 hours a day. It is a place where those who come here to spend time can truly begin to know how to live a life of love the way Christ taught when he said, "A new commandment I give unto you, that ye love one another as I have loved you, that ye also love one another." (John 13:24.)

It is also a place where all people can come together in work and play and lean how to live the Will of our Heavenly Father in their everyday lives. Heartlight Center is working toward being a living reality of God's Kingdom where people can come to experience a new, yet infinitely old way of life, a life of love, joy and peace.

Heartlight Center is located on 117 beautiful acres of wooded land with many lovely trails winding through its lush foliage. There are two fast-flowing streams of sparkling clear water and a serene emerald green lake which lies along the southern border of this sacred land. The entrance is about six miles west and north of Sturgis, Michigan.

There is an ongoing daily land program featuring meditation, reflection, service, relaxed time, exercises and vegetarian meals. Also, guided Land Tours and Quiet Visitations are available at any time upon request. If possible, please call ahead so that we might better receive you.

Services offered through Heartlight Center are as follows:

Services and Special Events-- Sunday Spiritual Services with concurrent Sunday School for children; Special holiday Celebrations; Peace Meditations; Family Service Programs; Spiritual Retreats, Classes, Workshops, covering topics from unfolding the Spiritual Self and Inner Transformation, to Meditation, Relationships, and Vegetarianism. All programs are offered on a free will donation basis, and seek to help each individual to understand and express more of their nature as a whole being of Light, physically, mentally, emotionally, and spiritually. We also have the vision of a noncompetitive, non-graded, wholistic, alternative school for children.

Community Care--There are several aspects to Community Care, all of which stem from the deep belief that we are here to care for one another, to help bring forth and nurture an atmosphere of cooperation, tolerance and love amongst all people. All services in Community Care are provided through volunteer efforts and are supported through community donations. The aspects of Community Care include services for the homeless (including housing, jobs, etc.), "Clothes for Kids" (providing warm winter outer wear for children), "Operation Hope" (providing basic needs, including food, household goods, furniture, assistance in planning low-cost, nutritious meals, and assistance in improving housecleaning skills, so that all might live in dignity), and most importantly, the opportunity, for those who have received services through Community Care, to give back to their community through volunteer services. It is truly "community helping community" in action.

Special Events--Christmas and spring celebrations, picnics,

children's program, etc. Heartlight is also very much involved in working for peace, from holding peace meditations on the land at special times, to working with other groups also interested in peace. Communication has begun between a Russian group and Heartlight to prepare for an exchange of pen pal letters between Russian and Heartlight children. We feel it is important to bring all nations together in love and children are very open to expressing love without regard to race, color or creed. The manifestation of peace is in everyone's hands.

Volunteer Work--Helping to serve the needs of the community. Heartlight has a community service program called "Helping Hands." It reaches out to serve in the community by bringing together those organizations which need volunteers and people who wish to volunteer. Their serving in the community brings a deep feeling of caring between those involved and will embrace everyone, for love has a way of touching every heart.

Literature--Diet, exercise, meditation and other lessons, a vegetarian cookbook, and other informational materials.

Weekly Classes--On a wide variety of selected subjects, from vegetarian cooking, diet and nutrition, aerobics, yoga to meditation, Bible study and the Laws of Creation.

We have a wonderful wholistic, fully-accredited, non-graded, non-competitive school (we already have the building). It will utilize the whole year by being in session for 45 days and off for 15 days. In the beginning it will be for children from Kindergarten through sixth grade. Children will learn individually as well as in a group situation. The challenge will be with the wonderful learning they experience rather than to be challenged through competition with each other. They will be taught to treat each other with love and kindness, to help each other and to live in peace together. They will be encouraged to reach to their highest potential and to express creatively in all areas. This way of learning will help them enter society fortified with all the strength, courage, compassion and understanding they will need to live successfully in the world, for the Heavenly Father takes care of all the needs of his children. These children will come to understand their connection with Him and the unlimited help He offers every step of the way.

If there is a calling in your heart for something more than what you are now experiencing and you are seeking answers to life's purpose and meaning, perhaps Heartlight can be of service. Please feel free to call or write. We will be happy to answer your questions and share with you our experiences on this wonderful journey called life.

HIGH WIND ASSOCIATION

**2602 E. Newberry Blvd.
Milwaukee, WI 53211
(414) 332-9503**

*"To walk gently on the earth
to know the spirit within,
to hear our fellow beings,
to invoke the light of wisdom, and
to build the future now."*

This credo expresses a vision that has drawn 300 Associates from around the country and abroad to support High Wind's experimental work in exploring ways of creating a more harmonious balance between people and nature. Most of this work takes place on a 46-acre farm on high rolling land in rural Wisconsin, 55 miles north of Milwaukee.

Drawing on earlier experiences with New Alchemy Institute, the Findhorn Community and Lorian Associates, the founders first organized a series of innovative seminars and conferences, often in conjunction with the University of Wisconsin.

High Wind's physical expression began in 1980 with a task group to build a "bio-shelter"--a passive solar residence with an attached research greenhouse. This evolved into a community, combining education with interests in ecology, shelter-building and renewable energy--all seen in the context of an overarching sacred intent. Our overall governance is by a board of eight, including some from the farm. Decisions about the functioning at the farm are made by the residents. Ten people live full or part-time at the farm (in four buildings), engaging in such activities as organic gardening and guest/learning programs.

High Wind operates the major alternative bookstore in Milwaukee and maintains a networking base in the city. Its substantive quarterly newsletter details the philosophy and challenges of daily life in the community, its gradual evolution toward a sustainable village (we're now acquiring an additional 20 acres), and the relationships between alternative models and mainstream culture.

Several private houses are being built--a commitment to High Winds into the foreseeable future. Other construction is anticipated as the community expands in scope and population; a process is in motion to place all the acreage into a land trust, with sites leased for individually built and owned homes and businesses. The trend is toward more decentralization, allowing people to live at High Winds in a number of ways: as long-term home owners contributing to the work of the whole; as staff responsible for ongoing programs and tasks; as volunteers or working guests experiencing High Winds for shorter periods; as specialists coming to create or participate in a particular High Winds-related project--such as an alternative school, a national think tank (The Plymouth Institute for New Policy), agricultural experiments; or as individuals wanting to pursue private artistic or economic initiatives in a sympathetic ambience. Such a diverse choice of agendas honors the different needs of people looking for various degrees of collectivity and privacy/autonomy within the framework of a shared philosophical base point. Members are financially responsible for their own support, often with jobs outside the community, but more recently also within High Winds as new entrepreneurial creativity unfolds.

HOHM

P. O. Box 4272
Prescott, AZ 86302
(602) 778-9189

The Hohm Community was founded in 1975 by Lee Lozowick, a Western Spiritual Master, and his students. Its main location is in the foothills of Arizona with "out reach groups" located throughout the United States and Europe (please refer to the list which follows). Our community is comprised of approximately 250 students and friends. It is intentionally kept small to allow direct interaction with the Master and a sense of bonding among community members.

Those of us attracted to the Hohm Community instinctually sought an alternative to the conventional way of viewing life, to the unconscious context/source from which life was habitually lived. Many of us may not have thought to intentionally seek the help of a living Spiritual Master, but have found it invaluable in our pursuit of a vibrant,"alive" relationship to God, to life.

We draw from all traditions and our daily lives include the practices of exercise, meditation, study, right relationship to diet (lacto-vegetarian) and sexuality (monogamous sexual relationship) and daily support of the community through work and financial contributions. We also strive for and emphasize sensitivity to others (adults and children!) and sensitivity to environment, to "spaces".

We attempt to carry a mood of celebration throughout our lives and hold formal gatherings, three times yearly. We also move to produce revelation through radical, direct, hands-on experiential work in travel, theatre and other art forms, as well as offer a "householder" lifestyle for those more drawn to that form.

The Hohm Community offers a range of possibilities for involvement ranging from casual interest in the Master's teaching to living in a community "group household" and beginning to practice the teaching, to actually engaging the Master directly on a daily basis by living with him on the main Ashram grounds.

We welcome questions, interest and correspondence. A prerequisite for visiting Hohm is the reading of our extensive introduction to our principles, practices and lifestyle which is titled Black and White and is available for $7.95, plus postage and handling, $10.00 total.

Contact any of our outreach groups for more information.

ARIZONA
Sedona, AZ
Bandhu Dunham
(602) 282-3215

CALIFORNIA
Claremont, CA
Rick Moore
(714) 625-2853

Los Angeles, CA
Wolfgang Dietrich
(213) 305-8860

San Rafael, CA
Greg Shaw
(415) 472-2868

Santa Cruz, CA
Shukyo Rainey
(408) 429-5036

COLORADO
Boulder, CO
Karl Rey
(303) 449-1205

Colorado Springs, CO
Jerry Page
(719) 633-0504

Denver, CO
Regina Sara Ryan
(303) 322-0360

FRANCE
Paris, France
Michelle Bonpois
011-331-4294-1023

GERMANY
Berlin, Germany
Martin Keck
030-6124322

Munich, Germany
Thomas Bormann
077-49-89-834-1520

NEW MEXICO
Santa Fe, NM
Bala Zuccarello
(505) 473-2028

JESUIT VOLUNTEER CORPS: NORTHWEST

P. O. Box 3928
Portland, OR 97208-3928

A Mission--For lay women and men to expore the meaning of the Gospel as they work full-time for social justice and peace.

An Opportunity--To share life with the poor and oppressed of the United States through direct service and advocacy.

A Challenge--to live simply and in community; to discover the causes of injustice; to integrate Christian faith and service.

The Jesuit Volunteer Corps was born as a daring adventure in lay outreach to Native American peoples in the Pacific Northwest and Alaska. During the 1970's, the Jesuit Volunteer Corps expanded to serve in both rural and inner-city settings across the country.

From our beginnings, the Jesuit Volunteer Corps has worked in collaboration with Jesuits, whose spirituality of linking faith and justice is incorporated into our work, community and prayer life.

After more than three decades of serving human needs in the spirit of our brave Alaskan beginnings, over 5,000 volunteers have been "ruined for life" as we say in the JVC.

The vitality of the JVC today comes from our continued commitment to work on the cutting edge of ministry with the poor. Hundreds of grassroots organizations across the country count on Jesuit Volunteers to provide essential direct services and advocacy with low-income people and with other persons who are marginalized in our society.

The JVC has a few job placements that require a specific credential or license. However, most JVC jobs can be done by people with a general educational background who have a willingness to learn new skills.

The values of spirituality, community and simple lifestyle are the cornerstone of JVC's commitment to social justice.

Spirituality--The JVC year is an opportunity for volunteers to explore and deepen their spiritual lives by integrating faith and work for justice.

Community--Jesuit Volunteers live with one another in a house, an apartment or in mission housing. Women and men come to JVC with diverse backgrounds and expectations. The challenge for each person is to respect and learn from these differences while building on common values.

Simple Lifestyle--JVC challenges each volunteer to live a simple lifestyle as a way of valuing people over things.

Jesuit Volunteers are placed in environments which encourage Christian growth and maturity through the discovery and development of each individual's gifts.

The Jesuit Volunter Corps offers: The challenge of Gospel values; Hard Work; Joy and frustration; Celebration; Practical job experience; Experiences of injustice and poverty; Lifelong friendships

The Jesuit Volunteer Corps encourages applications from people of all races and ethnic origins. Although the JVC is rooted in the Roman Catholic tradition, other Christian applicants are welcome.

Benefits--Room and board; Small monthly stipend; Health insurance; Deferred student loans; Tansportation home at the end of a year of JVC service; Orientation session, retreats, workshops and ongoing support by JVC staff.

Requirements--21 years old or older; Mature personality; Good health; College degree or work experience; Christian motivation.

Flexibility--Sense of humor; A willingness to be "ruined for life"; Applicants may be married (no dependents).

Costs--One-year commitment (begins in August); a few placements require a two-year commitment; No financial gain or loss; Losing an old self.

Interested people should contact the regional office of the area in which they would like to be placed.

The Jesuit Volunteer Corps--it's not just a job, it's an adventure!!!

JVC: Northwest
P. O. Box 3928
Portland, OR 97208-3928
(503) 228-2457
Alaska, Idaho, Montana, Oregon and Washington

JVC: Southwest
P. O. Box 23404
Main Office
1675 7th Street
Oakland, CA 94623-9991
(415) 465-5016
Arizona and California

JVC: South
P. O. Box 3126
Houston, TX 77253-3126
(713) 223-5387
Alabama, Arkansas, Florida, Georgia, Louisiana, Mississippi, New Mexico, South Carolina, Tennessee and Texas

JVC: Midwest
P. O. Box 32692
Detroit, MI 48232
(313) 894-1140
Illinois, Kentucky, Michigan, Minnesota, Missouri, Ohio and Wisconsin

JVC: East
Eighteenth & Thompson Streets
Philadelphia, PA 19121
(215) 232-0300
Connecticut, Maine, Maryland, Massachusetts, New Jeesey, New York, North Carolina, Pennsylvania, Rhode Island, Virginia, West Virginia and Washington, D.C.

KRIPALU CENTER
A Residential Experience of Conscious Living

Box 793, West Street
Lenox, MA 01240

Kripalu Center for Yoga and Health is a community of 220 men, women and children who live a holistic lifestyle expressly designed for self-transformation. Our community offers training programs to people from all over the world in such diverse areas as holistic health, yoga and massage. Our transformation comes through many different practices: through the work that we do, through the daily guided practice of yoga postures and meditation, through a balanced vegetarian diet, and through the direct teachings of our founder/director, Yogi Armit Desai.

An important foundation of our Center lies in the ancient science of yoga. Karma Yoga focuses on developing awareness through our 6-l/2 day work week. Whether we're repairing windows or chopping vegetables in the kitchen, we're learning the art of making every action a means to self-exploration and personal growth. As Genie Austin, a graphic designer from Pensacola, Florida writes, "At Kripalu I've learned to view any kind of work as an opportunity to challenge my creativity, efficiency,and imagination in a totally new way. The satisfaction of chopping vegetables into beautiful, clean, uniform pieces is really no different from that of designing a major publication. They joy is in the process, not the product."

Our day at Kripalu begins at 5 a.m. when we attend guided yoga and meditation sessions personally created by Yogi Desai to open body and mind. A balanced vegetarian breakfast follows at 6:30 a.m. after which we begin our seva (a yogic word meaning service (work)). We are a large community with many different skill needs--everything

from auto mechanics to computer operation. At Kripalu our intention is to learn to serve others without concern for external recognition or reward, and our work provides us a vehicle to cultivate this attitude of service.

Whether you're mopping floors or working on our grounds crew, every job contributes to your growth at Kripalu.

At noon we have an hour and a half break for lunch during which there are many different re-energizing activities available--such as tennis, swimming at our lake front beach, fitness workout in our weight room, sauna, whirlpool, aerobic dance and others. The emphasis in our lifestyle is on being balanced in all actions. Recreation balances our work schedule very well so that our 6-1/2 day work week never seems a drudgery. After lunch, our day continues until 5:30 dinner which is followed by free time. In the evenings, we meet as a group for satsang when the whole community comes together for singing and inspiration. We are in bed by 9:30 p.m. so we're

ready to begin another day at 4:30 the next morning.

We have had so much interest in our lifestyle from others that we have created a program called Spiritual Lifestyle Training, which allows people to come for a three-month* tuition-free work/study experience of Kripalu. This program allows a person to experience firsthand the benefits of living a holistic lifestyle as they work and live alongside our permanent residents. The lifestyle trainees are supported in their learning by weekly classes and workshops that teach the principles of personal and spiritual growth.

The Kripalu Center lifestyle works on all levels to bring about the gradual awakening of consciousness that is personal growth. A beautiful setting in the Berkshire Mountains, the inspiring teachings of Yogi Amrit Desai, and our special family of dedicated seekers, all add up to a unique learning environment. We invite you to write for more information.

Shorter time commitments are occasionally accepted.

LINDEN TREE COMMUNITY

**Rt. 2, Box 133
Underwood, MN 56586**

We are located in the lake country of west-central Minnesota, 20 miles northeast of Fergus Falls (pop. l2,000) and nine miles north of Underwood (pop. 600). The economy of our area is predominantly of two types: agricultural/dairy and tourism/recreation/fishing. Due to a high level of unemployment in the county, many people in this area attempt to create their own businesses or jobs.

Linden Tree (LTC) currently owns/uses roughly 80 acres of deciduous woodland and 10 acres of tillable farmland. All property is currently owned by individuals, but our stated goal in regards to our land is communal ownership. We are currently discussing various alternatives to meet this goal, including a cooperative land trust, private corporation, or a cooperative farm business.

We, as families, individuals, or couples, build our own homes and facilities. Currently there are three homes, a central community kitchen/living space, a workshop, guest house, chicken coop (40 members there), and a few small outbuildings. Future building plans include a large equipment machine shop, additional chicken space, a composting area, etc., etc. Quite often our building ideals outstrip our actual current abilities to create them, but they will happen.

We've just installed our first series of photovoltaic cells for electricity, and will have two buildings outfitted this winter. We have two deep wells that provide excellent water and irrigation. The third well (next spring) will be primarily for irrigation. We will be heating water with solar heat in the near future, although currently using wood for

heating and cooking. We are not anti-technology, but want to use it wisely and ecologically. Not much in the way of indoor plumbing yet.

We do not espouse any specific religious belief/spiritual path. Some of us are basically Christian, some agnostic, and some a combination of many forms of spirituality. We are open to all spiritual paths, but I think we value honesty, integrity, and basic humanism more than any dogma or labelled spirituality.

Currently we are engaged in a variety of economic ventures. As I mentioned earlier, this area is somewhat economically depressed, so if you're not a dairy/grain farmer, a resort owner, or a professional, (although all the above are having their own problems), making it economically is often a risky business. We prefer to develop our own business ventures, rather than working for someone or something. At the present we do rely on outside work/labor for financial support, but are definitely moving toward the preferred way. In l985, we will have a 6+ acre vegetable business, and have begun to develop a fairly stable marketing strategy for our products. We will be using organic, agroecological principles in a vegetable venture, and it is personally very exciting.

One member is currently in the early stages of developing a conservation/alternative energy business/dealership in the area. We have a wide variety of skills and knowledge among us, including bookkeeping, stonemasonry, carpentry, nursing, nutrition, farming, mechanical repair, and lots of good cooking!

Another venture in the early planning stage is the development of an educational/resource center using workshops, seminars, etc. for disseminating various forms of information/knowledge/ skills to people.

The possibilities are endless. Creating a better, more human world for ourselves, our children, and everyone else through example and education is most likely the paramount ideal of our community. As you can see, we are moving in a variety of directions at once. We have discussed the positive and negative aspects of this occasionally confusing life, but at the present feel that we want to explore many avenues of living and learning, and each new member/person will expand/clarify the direction(s) as we evolve. New members will be at the ground level of community building here!

We have been a community for 3+ years, and often talk of new members. We do have a few 'peripheral' members (very close friends) that visit for short periods of time. We are in the process of developing a criteria for new persons, but it's a tough one!

The criteria are not concrete by any means at the present, and we will welcome any/all suggestions. It may be that each new person(s) will be dealt with on a totally individual basis, with different needs for each.

Basic criteria somewhat agreed on so far include:

- be accepted by all community members

- no limitations to age, sex, race
- idealogically similar
- ability to help finance initial home/living space
- one year, non-member status
- families, couples or individuals

If you are definitely interested in more dialogue, we would like to hear from you! Send information about yourself, your own goals and directions, future plans and skills. Especially important to us are your thoughts/perspectives/feelings on community living and their relation to both what you need and what you have to offer. We would be happy to help arrange a visit from you. As the old saying goes: "A picture is worth a thousand words", or something like that. We'll be waiting for your reply.

MORNING STAR FARM, INC.

Ron and Donna Book
Berkeley, Ontario N0H 1C0
(416) 851-0139

Morning Star Farm, Inc. is a small rural cooperative community in central Ontario. We are a healthy, active and hardworking couple in our early 50's who have acquired 232 beautiful acres of scenic, rolling farmland with mature maple and cedar bushes, spring-fed trout stream, loam soil, and stone for building purposes. The buildings include an old, but livable, five-bedroom farmhouse, 408 ft. x 60 ft. metal-clad barn in excellent condition, several old outbuildings in need of repair, and four 18 ft. x 36 ft. buildings we have added ourselves. The property is located near Berkeley, Ontario, about 20 miles south of Owen Sound on a quiet and secluded, but easily accessible, concession road. We have obtained severances and approvals to build at least four additional residential structures. Our plans include self-sufficiency, alternative energy sources, private owner-built housing, shared use of common land, shops and equipment, innovative small-scale organic farming, greenhouses, cooperative enterprise, and cottage industry. etc. All we need now are four or five additional friendly, enthusiastic, committed and likeminded couples to invest skills, labor and some money to bring this dream into reality. If this sounds like what you are looking for, please write or call (in advance of any visit please) telling us about your own ideas, hopes, plans, and aspirations.

The Great Invocation

From the point of Light within the Mind of God
Let light stream forth into the minds of men.
Let Light descend on Earth.
From the point of Love within the Heart of God
Let love stream forth into the hearts of men.
May Christ return to Earth.
From the center where the Will of God is known
Let purpose guide the little wills of men--
The purpose which the Masters know and serve.
From the center we call the race of men
Let the Plan of Love and Light work out.
And may it seal the door where evil dwells.
Let Light and Love and Power restore the Plan on Earth.

MOUNTAIN GROVE COMMUNITY

**785 Barton Road
Glendale, OR 97442
(503) 832-2871**

A little over a year ago, I was sitting at our kitchen table mending clothes while contemplating on what this life is really all about. My innermost needs were not being met. I have a loving husband and two beautiful children, but I needed more.

I started thinking about how wonderful it would be to have a snug little cabin in the woods amongst other families that I really cared about. Someone to talk to while I was pulling weeds in the garden, someone to share a cup of coffee with while discussing what was happening in our lives, someone whom I could trust to watch my kids if I needed to run an errand, someone to share supper with and find out how their day went, someone to share my love, laughter and tears.

My husband shares these same dreams and, after discussing things we decided to put our house up for sale. We sent through the mail for the last issue of this directory and a little over 12 months and 2000 miles later we've found the land. Now we need to find the people!

We are hoping for a miracle in the next 12 months, but then we do believe in such things and much more. We believe people can live harmoniously with each other,

regardless of age, gender, or race, if they have the desire and spiritual fortification.

This article is written as an invitation to a dozen or so families or individuals looking to fulfill some higher needs. To list all these needs would be a repetition of many of these articles, for these needs are the common fabric behind all communities.

We are a non-profit organization with 400 acres of land located in southeast Oregon. 280 acres are selectively forested and the remaining 120 acres are agriculturally open to farming, but are presently meadows. There are over 13 miles of roads that allow access to most of the acreage, and a creek that meanders through the property providing potential irrigation or hydro-electric possibilities. We also have access to Interstate Highway 5 which is located only one block from the end of our driveway, although the freeway is not visible from any portion of the property.

There are some existing buildings available for housing; some with electricity and water, and others without either. All of these buildings will need some work and TLC, but could be a start for someone.

We have goals that need to be met in the next 12 months, first of which are our financial debts. There are enough funds to keep this place

afloat until the first part of 1990. The people we are looking for will have to be able to help share this financial debt with us and the other families that will live here. At this point in time w're pursuing the possibility of a Land Trust or 99-year lease option to offer a sense of security for everyone.

We hope this community will develop cottage industries, home schooling, concensus decision making processes, responsible land stewardship, energy self-sufficiency and be agriculturally self-sustaining.

Each new family or individual will have to build or remodel their own private residence, but hopefully we can share the evening meal in the large existing community building.

We feel to meet these goals will require a strong commitment from everyone. There will have to be open mindedness, autonomy, tenacity, a willingness to share both hopes and fears, and most important of all--the manifestation of ongoing spiritual growth.

As you can see, there are endless possibilities, and we are only as limited as our dreams. There's much to be done, one day at a time!

Through love and courage may you find what you seek!

If interested, please send a personal letter and SASE.

THE OJAI FOUNDATION

P. O. Box 1620
Ojai, CA 93023
(805) 646-8343

The Ojai Foundation is an educational and retreat center located on 40 acres of land in the Upper Ojai Valley. We endeavor to bring together the leading teachers from many different spiritual traditions, scholarly disciplines, and artistic pathways. What characterizes each of these teachers is a special quality of openness which allows them to meet one another and to explore to commonalities and points of convergence of their traditions. In this way, the Ojai Foundation operates on the model of the "empty chair" a gathering place where all the spokes on the wheel come together as equals. In doing so, we follow the 1927 vision of Dr. Annie Besant, who first obtained this land, and who foresaw the development of a unique educational center and community over 50 years ago.

What gives the Ojai Foundation its refreshingly distinctive quality is the harmonious interweaving of its three constituent parts--the educational program, the community, and the land itself. The programs provide a spiritual focus for personal and planetary evolution, at the same time reaching out to the larger circle of which we are a part. The community provides the context in which the teachings are translated into the nitty-gritty, day-to-day reality of living and working together, sharing the authentic challenges and celebrations of that process. The land provides the basic ground of the whole experience, allowing us to feel our connection to the Earth, and the wisdom, power, and beauty we can derive from that connection. These three aspects of the Ojai Foundation combine in a synergistic way to create a learning environment which is truly unique.

THE OJAI FOUNDATION
Work Scholar Program

"Now we must become warrior-lovers in the service of the Great Goddess Gaia, Mother of the Buddha. The stakes are all of organic evolution. Any childish thoughts of slipping off into Space must wait on this work--really of learning who and where we are, acknowledging the beauty, walking in beauty."--Gary Snyder

The Ojai Foundation offers the Work Scholar Program for those people interested in living close to the earth in a small community and working to support a diverse group of educational retreats. These retreats bring together leading teachers from many different spiritual traditions, scholarly disciplines, and the arts. Many retreats take place in the context of Council, an experimental format where teachers, staff and guests work, study, practice and celebrate together. This unique setting provides a challenging opportunity in which to learn and grow. Work scholars are called upon to balance community life, daily work rhythms, participation in retreats, and personal time within the context of a powerful natural environment and profound spiritual teachings.

There are three major components of the Work Scholar Program:

Supervised Work--The work experience is an integral part of the program. Work scholars are expected to work a minimum of 25 hours a week in one or more areas: kitchen, garden, office, Wild Store, or land crew, plus contribute to community maintenance.

Classes and Activities-- Work scholars may participate in Ojai Foundation retreats and ceremonies, as their work schedule permits. Ongoing activities include: Meditation, sweat lodges, and classes in the sacred traditions.

Personal Processing-- Work scholar meetings and personal consultations will be scheduled on an ongoing basis.

Participants in this program live close to the land and should be prepared for seasonal weather patterns. Work scholars are expected to provide their own tents, in addition to sleeping bag and personal equipment.

Work scholarships are available on a monthly basis for a fee of $375. Acceptance for an additional month is dependent on willingness to fulfill community responsibilities, timely payment of fees, and space availability. Please address all inquiries indicating your work skills, personal history, areas of interest, address and phone number to: Work Scholar Program, P. O. Box 1620, Ojai CA 93023.

PONDEROSA VILLAGE

Larry and Meg Letterman
195 Golden Pine
Goldendale, WA 98620
(509) 773-3902

A Self-reliant Lifestyle

We are deeply involved in a most interesting and demanding adventure--creating a satisfying place to live. The concepts behind the village are self-responsibility and independence, personal and spiritual growth, living and gardening with Nature, and voluntary cooperation. Land and homes are individually owned. This is neither a commune nor a cult. Some homesites are occupied, others are still available. It is a really nice place to be now--it can be a place of security (if needed) in the future.

A number of pioneers have joined us in the exciting job of creating this community. Currently there are 20 families and single people living here, for a total of 38 adults (ages 21 to 87) and 13 children (ages 6 months to 16). They are special people who have proven to be independent thinkers and self-starters with the incentive to take personal responsibility for shaping their own lives and their community rather than merely submitting to the prevailing forces. They come from a variety of backgrounds: engineers, carpenters, welders, sales managers, nurses, an aerospace scientist, cabinet maker, well driller, concession operator, lab technician, editor, secretaries, and teachers.

What Villagers are doing now to earn a living may have little to do with their former occupations. An aerospace engineer and his wife make very attractive jewelry boxes from driftwood and burls, selling them at crafts fairs all over the West. Another creates wood products for a local unfinished furniture manufacturer. Four Villagers work at Columbia Aluminum, a worker-owned plant. Several of the men construct or remodel houses. Two women are nurses at the nursing home in Goldendale, another is a medical receptionist/record-keeper. One couple started a business based on computer analysis that is so successful that it hires 10 others, some of them Villagers. One works as a printer in The Dalles. A former bank manager now does the accounting for a growing local business.

The architecture is as varied as the people and includes geodesic domes, earthbermed construction, a rammed-earth house, a house with a turret, a North German style timber frame, and others. There are twenty such homes already built or under construction here, each on its own five acre parcel. Most of the households have their own gardens and fruit trees. Keeping operational costs and efforts to a minimum makes the lifestyle here feasible.

The Village site is in south-central Washington State, 16 miles north of the Columbia Gorge and four miles from Goldendale, the County Seat of Klickitat County. The property is beautiful and peaceful with pines, firs, oaks, and grassy meadows. It is basically south-facing, with views of Mt. Hood (11,234 feet) and other 'snow-caps' visible from some places. Each of the five-acre parcels has been surveyed, all roads are constructed and some have all-weather surfacing. Utilities are available to a number of parcels.

Our community schedules Self-Reliant Life Seminars to help people explore the transition to rural self-reliant living, including earning a living, growing food organically, building energy-efficient houses, increasing our understanding of ourselves, others, and the environment.

We are looking for more participants--people of all ages with a variety of skills, knowledge, and resources--to move here and take part in the creation of our community. Those visitors are welcome who consider that they are able to buy a homesite, build their shelter (with shared help between themselves and other Villagers), provide the utilities they want, and realize the value of voluntary cooperation and interaction with those around them. A phone call or letter in advance of the visit is appreciated. There is ample camping space here, and there are grocery stores, motels and restaurants in Goldendale, four miles away.

Write for further information and Seminar schedule.

Villagers cooperate with each other in constructing homes.

RAINBOW RIDGE

A Residential Cooperative Community and Center of Education for Cooperatives and Peace

Jack & Connie McLanahan
3689 Berea Road
Richmond, KY 40475
(606) 623-0695

Member: U.S. Federation of "Educational Centers" for Cooperatives and Peace

Sponsor: Madison County Consumer-Owned Cooperative Society, Madison, Kentucky

Rainbow Ridge is 7.5 acres of high ground overlooking rolling farmland and cattle grazing on the hillsides, just east of I-75, six miles north of Richmond, 6 miles south of Berea, Kentucky, less than an hour south of Lexington. Jack and Connie McLanahan established a home there in the spring of 1984.

"Our goal", said the McLanahans, "is to develop a 'Residential Cooperative Community' that will serve as a 'Center' of Education for Cooperatives and Peace. This is not intended to be a religious community per se, though our values are grounded and nurtured by a quest to know God through all of the channels open to us. We participate in the Berea Society of Friends and the Interfaith Task Force for Peace and Justice. Our emphasis is on being a 'cooperative' community with extensive ties to the going world, rather than being a 'commune' or wholly 'intentional' community in the more narrow sense of those concepts as they are used today."

Rainbow Ridge is a member of the newly-formed U.S. Federation of Education/Strategy Centers for the Advancement of Cooperation and Peace. Other members are Sisu/olana Co-op Education Guild in Pomona, NY and Clasped Hands Education Center in Etna, California. Connie expresses their purpose in this manner: "Since there can never be peace without cooperation--instead of ever-increasing competition--and since the advantages and advancements in civilization come more from a wide variety of cooperatives than from the divisive capitalist system that appears to be ruining societies all over the world-- it is our hope that this network of Centers, reaching from California to New York, from Michigan to Kentucky will constitute a national cooperative "college experience" as influential in the U.S. as are the cooperative colleges in Canada, Scandinavia, England and on the Continent."

There is room for three other families at Rainbow Ridge, to work part time on Center programs, be responsible for the maintenance of their portion of the property and join with the others in taking care of common land and roads. Two families have expressed interest, but there have been no final commitments. To live and work congenially, families would have to have a clear philosophy of cooperation--values of the cooperative movement--and be educated to conflict resolution by peaceful means, both personally and internationally.

SHANNON FARM COMMUNITY

Rt. 2, Box 343
Afton, VA 22920
Attn: Jenny

We are a mixed group of people with overlapping goals and ideals. Together we own a 500-acre farm (purchased in 1974) just below the crest of the Blue Ridge Mountains in central Virginia. Presently, 44 adults and 14 children are Shannon members with all but eight living on the land. We move to and from the land according to our individual needs and the availability of housing.

As a group, we are committed to building a comprehensive alternative to the larger society. We favor organic use and care of the land, ecological concern, increasing our economic self-sufficiency, and eliminating sex roles and ageism. We are continually seeking to increase our skills in non-competitive decision-making. We reach decisions by consensus at our committee and monthly meetings, with a 60% majority vote used rarely to break deadlocks.

Although we share some common goals, no particular dogma, activity or spiritual base defines how we live.

For instance, although some Shannon members are vegetarians, we do not define Shannon as a vegetarian community. Likewise, we do not all follow the same spiritual path. As individuals, we lead diverse lifestyles. Some of us live alone, some in nuclear families and others in intentional groups. We enjoy this freedom of choices and feel it benefits us in at least two ways: people can change lifestyles and remain within the community;

and our diversity produces a dynamic evolving community.

Of our 500 acres, 350 are wooded, mostly mature hardwoods, and much of the rest is some of the finest river bottom farmland in Nelson County. The Rockfish River and several spring-fed streams run through the property. The terrain is a combination of flat land, meadows, hills, and mountain-sides.

Rather than scatter houses over the land, we now have six designated cluster areas for housing. We agree on building plans as a group. This encourages thoughtful structures which are in harmony with the environment and our group needs. We have built 18 houses, as well as a wood shop, solar lumber kiln and warehouse. Also, we have a community house and a large hay barn.

The land, houses, and other buildings are owned by Shannon Farm Association, Inc., a non-profit corporation controlled by all the full members. Financing for building construction is the responsibility of individuals, who hold long term leases on the completed structures.

Some members work in nearby cities like Charlottesville (25 miles away), and other members work on the land. Since most of us want to work within the community, we create our own work collectives. Heartwood Design, the woodworking and construction collective, now employs 10 members full or part time. Starburst, our computer collective, involves six members in progamming and integrating small business computers. Health, social services, insurance, teaching, food services and advertising are among the other professions in which members are employed.

In the agricultural area we have members involved in a small truck farm and a nursery which features edible landscaping. Other projects include gardening, an orchard, horses, a milk cow, chickens, and beekeeping. Off the land, we're also involved with an alternative school and a food co-op.

Joining Shannon as a provisional member requires the support of 1/3 of the membership. After six months to a year, a provisional member can become a full member with the support of 2/3 of the membership. Full members pay 7% of their monthly income, after taxes, in dues and contribute labor. Provisionals pay 5% and labor. There is no capital investment requirement; however the initial purchase of the land was made possible by substantial loans from many members and further loans are needed. These loans are gradually being paid off with our dues income.

To join Shannon in a more real sense requires the establishment of bonds with existing members. This happens as mutual areas of interest are explored and people get to know one another. Most living groups are open to new people and our work collectives are vital in bringing new and old members closer. None of this is automatic, however. It's up to prospective members to find jobs and a place to live. Of course, we help each other more and more as the personal bonds develop.

We want to emphasize that we are an evolving and diverse community. We are seeking members of all ages, races, and sexual orientations. We welcome those who are seriously committed to the values evident in our endeavor: those who want to help build Shannon!

SIRIUS COMMUNITY
Sirius Service Programs

Baker Road
Shutesbury, MA 01072
(413) 259-1251

Sirius Community, named after the star known esoterically as the source of love and wisdom for the planet, was begun in 1978 on 86 acres of land by former members of the Findhorn Community in Scotland. Today we are about 20 Full Members from many spiritual paths, and 10 children. We have many Associate Members across the country and the world.

What draws us here and holds us is a vision, first outlined by the founders, filled in by all of us, molding us even as we mold it. It is a vision to attain the highest good in all levels of God's creation--field and forest, plants and animals, humans and angels, earth and stars.

The spiritual understandings we strive to embody have been lived by visionaries in all cultures down through the ages: faith in God, love, truth, cooperation, honoring the oneness of all life, detachment from desire, meditation, and service to the world. We at Sirius, a group of diverse people from different backgrounds, who are working to respect and appreciate our differences, yet joyfully cooperate. What we are doing can be applied globally, for the tensions between nations pose a similar challenge.

Our method is simple: in any polarity or conflict, we work to create balance and focus on the wholeness of the system, rather than the separateness of the parts. The tools we use include a weekly meeting and open discussion by all adult members, governance by group meditation and consensus, attunement to God, to nature and to each other. We strive to balance an interconnectedness permitting us to live close to the earth without being bound to it. For us, "appropriate technology" is computers, as well as composting toilets and wood stoves.

We also strive toward right livelihood, earning our living through loving, non-exploitive ways. A few of us work at Sirius or in our own businesses, but most of us are employed outside the community. We work in such fields as social and health services, solar construction, whole foods distribution, domestic service, socially responsible investment, media, publishing and educational services.

We grow some of our vegetables and build our own houses. We share equally the expenses of the land and work on community projects one day a week. Most of us participate in community evening meals and a food buying club.

We seek to meet the world's needs by welcoming visitors from many countries into our kitchens to share our meals, into our sanctuary to share our group meditations, and onto our construction sites to share with us in creating solar buildings. We make ourselves available to those on a spiritual quest and those in transition seeking a better life. As a non-profit, tax-exempt educational center, we offer a variety of educational programs, from solar construction to spiritual science, from organic gardening to wholistic heal-ing. Each Sunday we offer a spiritual service, and on the first and third Sundays of the month, an open house.

More importantly, we serve the world through our meditation. We work to create positive thought-forms of peace and healing for the world, as we know that energy follows thought. We are striving together to build Sirius as a center of Light, a place where cooperation is a dream that works. We see our service as helping to build a Network of Light radiating positive energy and hope for the future throughout the world.

Community Experience

The members of Sirius Community invite you to visit, and join us for a community living experience as we work together to build a better world. We begin our workday, renamed "joyful productivity" at 9:00 a.m. on Saturday with a meditative attunement. This brings our attention and energy to the present, in coordination with each other and the Divine. The day's activity may include cooking, helping build our new community center, cleaning, doing office work, gardening and any other tasks we undertake as a group. These activities allow all of us to get to know each other through our shared work experience.

Please call or write in advance of your visit, or for information about programs, subscription to our quarterly Journal or Associate Membership.

SPIRAL

P.O. Box 337
Monticello, KY 42633

Spiraland is 250 acres in the foothills of south-central Kentucky, in the Cumberland Valley. Covering a ridge and valley of forest and cleared land, Spiral includes 3 springs, a good barn, an old log cabin, and the new dwellings wimmin are building.

Spiral wimmim have chosen to incorporate as a Land Trust, a non-profit organization holding title to the land in stewardship for present and future generations of wimmin. The land is held "in perpetuity," for all time, and the Trust is committed to nurture, conserve, and maintain the resources and abundant life of this small portion of Mother Earth.

Spiral Wimmin recognize that the land is a sacred heritage belonging to herself, part of the complex web of life in which we may learn to play our part harmoniously with the rest of her creatures and plants.

Spiral wimmin's community is based on Permaculture principles. Our actions on the land are to enhance the diversity and abundance of life forms, to preserve and build the soil, to work with the cycles and forces of nature. We look at the land as a self-sustaining ecological system capable of fruitfulness for all time.

Spiral wimmin form a web that stretches from coast to coast, promoting feminism and challenging sexism, racism, ageism, ablism, capitalism, and heterosexism in our patriarchal society. Feminism advocates for wimmin the social, economic, spiritual, and political freedom to determine our own lives. We encourage and support each other in freeing ourselves in order to create wimmin's culture, spirituality, and community.

Spiral Wimmin's Land Trust leases to wimmin committed to being part of a community striving for self-sufficiency and based on cooperation and consensus decision making.

Spiral Wimmin's Community welcomes visitors and new members.

Community Members are those who intend to or are living on Spiraland, with the financial and social commitments to make Spiral work.

Supportive Members can participate in building a cooperative wimmin's community, and encourage Spiral growth by--

- attending events on the land
- camping, visiting, working
- networking and serving on committees and projects
- contributing $3/1000 of yearly income, or $1000 Lifetime, subject to land use fees/work exchange.

If you are interested, please write or call and tell us how you connect in the web.

THE TEACHING DRUM OUTDOOR SCHOOL

P. O. Box 1892
Eagle River, WI 54521
(715) 479-9292

We are a community of teachers and support people who teach aboriginal skills and awarenesses in a wilderness environment, presenting them as tools to explore and become more attuned to our inner and outer selves. We are the evolution of Coldfoot Creek, a Wisconsin northwoods community of 20 that disbanded last year.

Incorporated as a non-profit school, we offer classes in crafts and skills, native lifeways and spirituality, nature writing, natural swimming techniques and canoe treks. We also write and publish related educational materials.

Our Purpose

Our purpose is to provide learning opportunities inspired by age-old wisdoms and ways of living in balance with each other. By honoring these ways, we are better able to achieve balance in our contemporary lives and to more fully partake in the care and healing of our common mother, the earth.

Our Name

The drum is the only universal musical instrument. For earth peoples, it is the symbolic center--the organizing point of their social, political, and spiritual lives. In this sense, the word drum refers to a group of people drawn together for a common purpose. The beat of our hearts and the pulse of the earth echo in the beat of the drum as we work together toward achieving balance.

Teaching Methods

The Old Way's approach to teaching differs from most contemporary approaches; its goals and perceptions reflect an entirely different way of living and of looking at the world. At the Teaching Drum, we learn in the Old Way. Contemporary teaching methods often focus on intellectual survival skills that ignore the development of senses and instincts. These parts of us are devaluated in a culture characterized by dependence on mass media and machines rather than use of them as tools.

Further, our culture fosters a way of life in which we emphasize sanitation and personal cleanliness, yet we pollute our water, air, and soil. We are living as though we are separate from each other and from the earth.

In the Old Way, however, we are whole beings whose intellects function in balance with our instincts and senses. We are no longer separate within ourselves or from those who surround us. Instead, the Old Way emphasizes the interdependence between earth and its creatures.

In the natural realm, learning and living are not separate. A young wild animal acquires hunting skills within the greater context of its life. In keeping with this way, at the Teaching Drum we present skills in context with their use. For instance, bow and drill firemaking is not

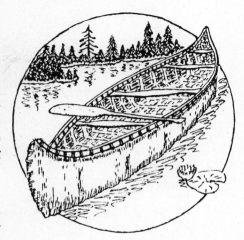

taught as an isolated lesson, but as a means to keep warm on the canoe trail, make a smokeless fire, and prepare wild foods.

Also in the Old Ways, the roles of teacher and student are not divided. Both learn and both teach. The teacher brings experience, the student, new perspective; and the student learns, not only through the wisdom of the teacher--the external guide but also through the Coyote--the internal teacher, the inquisitive voice within.

Learning in the Old Way allows both involvement with the self and immersion in the environment. The ultimate goal is to achieve both personal balance and balance within the greater circle of existence. At the Teaching Drum Outdoor School, our goal mirrors that of the Old Way. We wish to discover ourselves by reestablishing and strengthening our connection with the earth and its creatures.

Openings

We are looking for two or three people to join us, to serve as apprentices for approximately six months, then assume staff positions. We also have an opening for a gardener, to propagate the Old American Native vegetable varieties we've been collecting and preserving. And we'd like to have an articulate and key-board-literate person join us, to handle correspondence, mailing list updates, light bookkeeping, and the coordination of activities for students and staff.

We all work together here, as our small size and closeknit structure minimize strict divisions of labor and involve us in many aspects of the Teaching Drum.

For more information, a copy of our newsletter and course brochure, please send us your address and two 25-cent stamps.

TERAMANTO

10218 147th S.E.
Renton, WA 98056
(206) 255-3563

Fifteen miles east of Seattle in semi-rural May Valley Co-op Community (MVC) lies Teramanto ("Loving Earth"-- Esperanto) Community. Along nearby trout and salmon coursing May Creek, wild geese, duck, quail and an occasional deer come. Horses roam the wide pastures. All enjoy the country clean air and quietness.

MVC is 15 homes on one-third acre lots surrounded partially by 21 acres of MVC forest, creek, barn, and five-plus acres of pasture, garden and orchard. Teramanto (Tera), an autonomous community within MVC, includes three adjacent houses, another lot and one and one-half acres of the pasture. Two of the houses have been home to two small families for over nine years. The third, occupied since 1982, has been home for anywhere from three to eight persons (families and/or singles.)

Tera started in '74 as an intentional community. It has been organized by A Pacific Group (APG) formed in 1970 by Fellowship of Reconciliation members. (FOR is the oldest religiously motivated, non-denominational pacifist organization of the West.) However Tera's philosophy and purpose have been developed over its life. They are: faith in the future- -in God or order in the universe and in every person; love (giving or service) to Humankind--associates and acquaintances especially; and the greater social effectiveness of channelling one's love through one's community.

Carrying out this philosophy happens in different ways. One is through generous service to each other and in such kindred organizations as the Puget Sound Cooperative Federation, military tax refusal and other peace activist groups, Tilth (organic agriculture), alternative energy associations, and co-ops. Now Tera is sponsoring formation of a land trust for intentional communities and for preservation of open space. Tera's main contribution, though, is maintaining an open door to new residents---expanding and perhaps later forming a rural daughter community.

Another way is through what has been called voluntary simplicity, i.e. reducing one's own needs in order to better meet the needs of others. Tera aims to meet them by producing goods and services in an environment of love, joy and support--for internal use and for barter. An important by-product of these endeavors has been the personal growth in skills and character of the residents.

Progress toward economic autonomy has been mostly through subsistence production:

- Organic use of the community garden and orchard and two solar greenhouses are being prepared for winter production. Surplus has gone to neighbors and the Food Bank.

- A beehive is in production and is being expanded.

- Firewood is obtained from the MVC forest for the total heating needs of two houses.

There are also two income-producing enterprises operated by residents from their homes. Both provide work to other Tera residents. Other income-producing enterprises such as solar home construction and a tool co-op run by residents are planned.

Tara is open to all in agreement with its purposes and philosophy. Newcomers first live and work with Tera folks for four to six days. If that trial succeeds they may stay for up to six months, subject to mutual agreement. After a similar second six months they may apply for membership. Membership confers equal voice in basic (consensus) decisions, permanent residence, and priority on benefits. Non-members participate in an advisory capacity.

Residents each share the work of the community (part-time). They likewise share a part of their outside income, over $100 a month, to meet Tera cash expenses. Those without sufficient outside income may qualify for a cash allowance. All real property in Tera is practically debt-free and is corporately owned. Members are required to invest what they can afford in Tera, it being returned when they leave. Visitors are welcome by advance appointment. Contact us for more details.

TRAILS END RANCH

R. R. 2, Box 924
Royal, AR 71968

We spent seven years of research and 100,000 miles of camping and visiting before we decided on our area in Arkansas. Many states were investigated 3-4 times in conjunction with our shopping list of pluses and minuses. After deciding on this 40-mile circle in the Quachita National Forest we were fortunate to find one of the loveliest places we had seen near the forest with mountains on three sides, rolling hills with tall trees, pasture, pond, and a large garden area. We have a view in all directions from our secluded location. We are 11 miles from Hot Springs, a town of 36,000 with all necessary stores, clubs, retail establishments, etc.

Our eventual goal is to have a complete lodge-type community that would have "out" residences. We have formed our group around a modified-extended family lifestyle. We wish everyone to like and be concerned with the problems and emotions of the others and a willingness to help or pitch in. We believe a small group can have more interaction and commitment to each other and thus provide more time for pursuit of our personal goals and our group interests such as camping, traveling, social action and environmental programs. This lifestyle will reduce over-all living expenditures, general overhead and enable us to pursue community projects. We are a non-sectarian group with no political right or left wing tendencies and generally try to conduct ourselves and our cottage industries without the needless interference of the establishment.

To those not familiar or having time to study 15 or 20 states, our part of Arkansas lies in the center of a 40-mile pocket intertwined by three rivers, three major lakes and two mountain ranges. The additional advantage is that travel from this central location in the U.S. can be in all directions without considerable length of time.

We have developed several exclusive cottage industries that would enable key people to earn an income without leaving the grounds. We are an easy-going group interested in furthering our education and hobbies which would include some work, play, travel and development of an environmental program.

We feel communication via correspondence is essential to establish an understanding of your desires and our activities prior to a visit. We are truly interested in additional people who are sincere, honest, of any age, who want to explore this unique and unusual lifestyle.

A brief resume and background data and a picture certainly is of great value to help us accelerate the visitation process.

Thanks again for your inquiry and we look forward to hearing from you. Please let us hear from you.

Sincerely in love and peace, Trails End Ranch

TRUTH CONSCIOUSNESS
Sacred Mountain Ashram

3305 County Road 96
Ward, CO 80302
(303) 447-1637

"All the forces and movements of life should be regulated and directed toward that one Goal which gives all the satisfaction, peace and bliss. All other relations, possessions and viewpoints should be consecrated to and sanctioned by Divine Will." -- Swami Amar Jyoti

Pujya Swamiji often speaks of "New Age Consciousness". Because the term has been used in an ever-widening context, He clarifies the New Age as the uplifting of human consciousness into a life in tune with the Divine. Whatever we may create, either as individuals or as a society, that does not point us toward that Perfection will always leave us dissatisfied with life. It will leave us searching, consciously or unconsciously, for the fulfillment that lies within. We may call it Love or Consciousness, Rama, Krishna, Jesus, Buddha, or simply Light. Until we merge with that we will never stop seeking.

In 1961, when Swami Amar Jyoti came down from Himalaya, He traveled in pilgrimage the length and breadth of India. Seeing His radiant wisdom lit from within, many were attracted to follow Him. To satisfy their longing, He found Jyoti Ashram in Pune and later in Delhi (India). In 1961, He was invited by a disciple to accompany him to America. Traveling inconspicuously in the United States, more devotees were attracted to His Presence. But it was not until 1973 that he returned to the U.S. and eventually founded three more ashrams--outside Boulder (Colorado), Tucson (Arizona) and Rockford (Michigan). In 1988, Prabhushri Swamiji opened a heavenly new abode for Sacred Mountain Ashram at 9,400 feet elevation with nine gla-

cial lakes reflecting the majestic snow ranges of the Colorado Rockies.

Traditionally, an ashram is the home of the Guru where sincere aspirants may come for Darshan or guidance, and also dwell there in His/Her Light. The Master knows the temperament of each soul and guides him or her on their natural path to the Goal. Public programs, which all those sincerely interested may attend, include Satsangs (Spiritual Discourses), meditation and yoga classes, and retreats held several times during the year. The ashrams also provide a place where devotees may serve in the spirit of karma yoga (selfless service) which purifies the body, heart, and mind. In 1981, two Truth Consciousness Community Centers were established where seekers from all walks of life, including families, may live a God-centered life. Truth Consciousness produces tape recordings of the Satsangs of Swami Amar Jyoti, as well as Chants to the Divine that are sung by ashramites and devotees and recorded live at Satsangs. Publications include Swamiji's highly acclaimed books: *Retreat Into Eternity*, *Spirit of Himalaya - the Story of a Truth Seeker*, and *In Light of Wisdom*. Each beautifully produced

book is a jewel of ageless wisdom. Other publications include the thrice-yearly *Light of Consciousness Journal*, full of color posters and note cards, and calendars. A stunning 1990 calendar has been published this year. Beautiful color photography and the words of Swami Amar Jyoti lead you on an inspiring pilgrimage within.

The heart and core of Prabhushri's work, however, is not the center or publications. He has always clearly stated that the institution is merely a vehicle for spiritual awakening. It is the intense, personal attention given to each seeker who sincerely aspires to the Goal that Swamiji says He is here for. He gives no "religion", for He says that the time of religions is drawing to a close. It is for the freedom of the soul that He has come. The focus of all programs, practices, services and relationships at Truth Consciousness centers is the common goal of Truth, devotion to God and Guru and Enlightenment. Guests are welcome to visit or stay at the centers by special arrangement. While there is no fee for any of these services, other than retreats, donations are always welcome.

DIRECTORY

On the following pages you will find a compilation of intentional communities. Over 800 communities were invited to submit listings. Those who responded are those who are ready to announce their existence to others. Some chose not to be listed for many reasons: because the response is sometimes overwhelming and correspondence hard to keep up with (some groups are too small to handle the number of visitors a public statement like this brings); others are full to capacity or prefer to remain unpublicized; while still others are in stages of transition or undetermined status.

Following are some suggestions for contacting and visiting communities. Of course, these are generalizations, as each community has its own protocols for visitors. To find out about specific communities, please contact them well in advance of the time when you wish to pay them a visit. Most of these suggestions are just plain common courtesy.

1. If you are writing for information, please include a self-addressed stamped envelope. A small donation, if you can afford it, is always appreciated.

2. If you are calling a community, please do not call collect.

3. Most communities are the homes of the members. "Drop-ins" may meet with a less-than-warm reception.

4. Do not use communities as a "crash pad" on your trips from here to there. Such curiosity seekers are not looked on kindly by most community members.

5. Most communities do not have sleeping/cooking facilities for guests. Please find out particulars in advance. You may need sleeping bag/camping gear.

6. Leave your pets at home.

The following suggestions have come to us from several communities:

1. In writing to communities do not send an inquiry like this: "Dear ___, please send me more information about your community. Sincerely, XXX". Many communities do not respond to these letters. They don't have the time or the energy. They do answer even xeroxed letters that tell something about the inquirer, who he/she is and what is sought.

They do answer thoughtful questions, and like letters in which folks talk about themselves.

2. When you receive information from a community, please acknowledge their reply, even if you are no longer interested.

3. If you are planning to move soon, or if you should change addresses midstream in a series of communications with a community, please leave a forwarding address. No one likes to feel they are spending their valuable time and energy on correspondence which is being sent off into outer space!

A note to communities: Some of these suggestions work two ways...We often receive distressing letters from folks who take the time and energy to pour out their hopes, dreams, and autobiographies in letters to communities only to anxiously await replies that never come. So communities...Please be courteous and reply to heartfelt inquiries!

If communities and seekers alike try to follow these guidelines, keeping in mind respect for their fellow human beings, the river of communication will flow much smoother and all will benefit from the interaction.

In contacting communities, if you should find that any have moved, closed down, or are no longer seeking new members, we would appreciate you dropping us a line and letting us know so we can cross them out of the directory. In this way you can help others so they won't waste their time writing dead-end letters.

UNITED STATES

ARIZONA

ARCOSANTI

I-17 at the Cordes Junction Exit
HC 74, Box 4136
Mayer, AZ 86333
(602) 632-7135

"As urban architecture, Arcosanti is probably the most important experiment undertaken in our lifetime."--Newsweek

Est. 1970. Urban community under construction at Cordes Junction, central Arizona. Inspired by Paolo Soleri. Based on "Archology" (architecture and ecology), it offers an alternative to current urban dilemmas by reorganizing a sprawling urban landscape into a dense, integrated, three-dimensional town. When completed will be a 25-story structure, heated by a four-acre food supplying greenhouse. Of a total 860 acres, 846 will remain in their natural state or be used for farming or recreational needs of the projected 5,000 person community. Forty resident members guide students and professionals who pay about $500 to participate in five-week construction workshops where they learn skills and the joys of accomplishment.

Arcosanti intends to become a human laboratory where on a modest scale the fundamental tenets of Archology will be tested. At the present time only about 2% of construction has been completed.

CHILDREN OF THE LIGHT

Star Rt. Box 39
Dateland, AZ 85333

Christian community located on 80 acres with many amenities. We are vegetarians, and the purpose of this communal way of life is to establish a new system--Christ's Kingdom way on earth. We do not solicit new members, but fully believe that those who come will be led here by the Spirit of God. Children are welcome as well; it is for whosoever will desire to dedicate their lives wholly unto the Lord.

(Please see "Articles" section of this book for more information.)

COOPER STREET HOUSEHOLD

Triangle F Cooperative
Box 238
Vail, AZ 85641

Organization--We are a cooperative intentional household. Our structure is loose. Few rules seem needed, but tolerance for the life-styles of others is expected. Everyone contributes money and work, but this differs according to circumstances. Most plans evolve informally but everyone is consulted on matters that affect them. Consensus is used for major decisions such as the acceptance of a new family member.

Central Theme/Purpose--Basically we feel that we can lead a better life together, living in community, than separately. Financially we are certainly better off; emotionally we appreciate and need others. We are not held together by common work, religion, a belief system or cultural background. Most of us have full personal lives in the surrounding community and our own individual sets of friends and activities. There are some common themes, however. We all reject the culture around us as absurd, pathological and immoral.

Membership--Currently (Spring, 1989) we are five adults. We range in age from 25 to 60. All work outside in the community.

Physical Setting--Our community has two locations. One is a suburban home in Tucson. The other is a 22-acre "ranch" in an isolated canyon 35 miles away, in the foothills of the Rincon Mountains. Our little ranch has water and electricity. We garden and raise chickens and ducks.

THE GLOBAL ORDER

4220 N 25th St.
Phoenix, AZ 85016
(602) 468-0605

Established in 1954, the Order has provided the volunteer staff of both the Ecumenical Institute and the Institute of Cultural Affairs (ICA). The Institutes have offices in 35 countries around the world. There are residential communities of the Order in more than 25 of these locations and the members represent many national, religious, and cultural backgrounds.

The center in Phoenix is the coordinating center for communities located in Oklahoma City, Denver, Seattle, and Phoenix. Its facility consists of a 17-unit apartment complex in a quiet residential neighborhood. Members of the community share food, housing, health care and some child care expenses. The couples, singles, and families which make up the community join in shared work, recreation, study and celebrational activities.

Some members of the community work full time for ICA West, while others work for other organizations and may volunteer time with the ICA. The ICA has developed methods which encourage people to participate in creating their own future. These methods have been used extensively in self-help community development, organizational transformation and in educational methodologies. They enable team and consensus building and participatory planning/decision making. The methods of the ICA are also used extensively in the common life of the community.

In the Western states there are some 70 people who are structurally part of the Order community even though only 30 of them live in the four residential community settings. There are an additional 200 people who have been a part of the community and continue to be closely affiliated.

THE HOHM COMMUNITY
P. O. Box 4272
Prescott Valley, AZ 86302

A community founded by a Western Spiritual Master, Lee Lozowick, and his students, Hohm offers the possibility of a vibrant, alive relationship to God, to life, through direct relationship to a living Spiritual Master, with a strong foundation of daily practice, drawing from all religious traditions with an emphasis on eastern traditions. We welcome questions and correspondence regarding our work and have recently published an extensive introduction which can be purchased through us.

(See "Articles" section.)

NORTHEON FOREST
10200 N. Camino Valdeflores
Tucson, AZ 85737

(See listing in Pennsylvania.)

"If in the twillight of memory we should meet once more, we shall speak again together and you shall sing to me a deeper song. And if our hands should meet in another dream we shall build another tower in the sky."--The Prophet

REEVIS MOUNTAIN SCHOOL OF SELF-RELIANCE
HCO 2, Box 1534
Globe, AZ 85501

We are a New Age, vegetarian, self-reliant community and school. We are dedicated to teaching, native herbology, natural healing and health, metaphysical philosophy, outdoor self-reliant skills, compassion for the Earth and the family of humankind. We are open to new members, including children, but with discretion. Prospective members must be like-minded and should first communicate by mail. Write for a free class brochure. Our weekend and one-week courses include: wilderness doctoring, herb study classes, practical herbology, stone masonry, wilderness survival skills, spirituality simplified, tai chi chuan.

We're located near Globe, Arizona, but for more information, contact our Phoenix Representative: Deborah Peterson at 4218 N. 49th Dr., Phoenix, AZ 85031 - (602) 252-6019.

ARKANSAS

CROSSES CREEK YOUTH RANCH AND CHRISTIAN COMMUNITY
R R 2, Box 185-A
Elkins, AR 72727
(501) 643-2338

Crosses Creek Youth Ranch is a spiritual community of adults and children living together, united by cooperation and respect for each other.

Located in the midst of the scenic Ozarks and on the White River.

The community is supported by community-owned businesses such as carpentry, crafts, greenhouse, gardening, print shop, and some members work at jobs outside the community.

We are looking for financially responsible, dedicated, sincere, and hard-working people. We do not allow the use of alcohol or drugs.

TRAILS END RANCH
R.R. 2 Box 924
Royal, AR 71968

Established 1981, a small group of like-minded people interested in physical and emotional well-being and environmental development. Operating under a modified extended family lifestyle of work-sharing and social equality, blended with nature, natural foods and development of our personal goals. Our mountainous location near the National Forest encompasses 3 lakes, rivers, hiking trails and unlimited adventure in the 1-1/2 million acre park. Our cottage industries are thriving and we look for several more sincere, honest and thoughtful people to fill out our group. All replies welcome. (See "Articles" section for more information.)

CALIFORNIA

3HO INTERNATIONAL HEADQUARTERS
Guru Ram Dass Ashram
P. O. Box 35006
Los Angeles, CA 90035
(213) 550-9043

The 3HO Foundation (healthy, happy, holy) is an international educational and spiritual organization exemplifying the standards of righteous living and service to humanity that is the foundation of the Sikh Dharma (founded in India during the 15th century).

3HO offers classes in Kundalini Yoga, Tantric Yoga, meditation, and other subjects aimed at improving the quality of one's life experience. Gatherings, courses and camps are open to all.

3HO communities require no vows nor "initiations", but serious students commit themselves to daily routines of yoga and meditation, hard work to earn an honest living, and active sharing for the group.

Other headquarter locations:

East Regional Headquarters--Guru Ram Dass Ashram, 1740 White Wood Lane, Herndon, VA 22070 (703) 435-4411

Canada--Guru Ram Dass Ashram, 346 Palmerston, Toronto, Canada M6G 2N6 (416) 964-0612

European Regional Headquarters--Guru Ram Dass Ashram, Den Texstraat 46, Amsterdam, Holland 10 17 zc tel: 24-19-77

ALCYONE LIGHT CENTRE
c/o 2139 Old Stage Rd.
Hornbrook, CA 96044
(916) 475-3310

Small group of people in a residential community on magnificent land on Oregon/California border with view of Mt. Shasta. Beginning to build. Need gardeners, foresters, builders. Ultimate goal is to become a Planetary Village. Share a creative spiritual adven-

ture balancing heart/mind energies to enhance life as a co-creative enterprise in harmony with all life. Also a strategic link with other communities around the planet. People encouraged to pursue their own path, but family meditation mandatory. School of Sacred Architecture courses available once a month. Resident Wellness--total health program commencing Fall, 1985 (ongoing, as integral part of the Educational Centre). Community is located near Ashland, Oregon.

APPLETREE COMMUNE
P. O. Box 5
Cottage Grove, OR 97424
(503) 942-4372

One-household community. Currently three adults and one child on 23 acre homestead. We plan to grow to 10-20 members. We practice organic gardening and are interested in permaculture, and plan to have chickens and goats. Communal businesses--computer programming, tie dye, day care. Some members hold outside jobs. We're interested in new cottage industries. Ecological lifestyle--mostly vegetarian diet. Communal child raising--plan to homeschool. Emphasis on open communication. Income and property sharing. Middleground decision-making, backed up by consensus minus one, two or three votes, depending on our size. Work credit system with quota and personal allowance. Member of Federation of Egalitarian Communities. We are seeking members--adults, children, babies welcome. Visitors welcome; write first. Send $1.00 for booklet on all Federation Communities.

ANANDA COOPERATIVE VILLAGE
14618 Tyler Foote Rd.
Nevada City, CA 95959
(916) 292-3494 or 292-5877

A yoga-oriented community of 200+ adults and kids in a rural setting, Ananda is 17 years. old and growing. Members are disciples of Yogananda (*Autobiography of a Yogi*); leader of community is Swami Kriyananda (*The Path*). Central business is year-round guest meditation retreat that offers classes in yoga, meditation, healing, spiritual relationships, and more (send for program guide). Also organic garden, dairy, clothes shop, vegetarian cafe, publications. Products include music and talk tapes, incense/oils, books (spiritual, postures, cooking--send for catalog). Spiritual schools K-12. Residential centers throughout California and in Italy. Worldwide meditation groups.

THE AQUARIAN MINYAN

P. O. Box 7224
Berkeley, CA 94707
(415) 848-0965

New Age egalitarian Jewish spiritual community, meets weekly as a portable Shul in people's homes. Shabbos, Holyday & Festival celebrations combine traditional prayers and songs with innovative liturgies, dance, storytelling, and other more personal sharing. Also sponsors workshops, particularly in Jewish mysticism and related topics. Newcomers and non-Jews welcome. Newsletter available.

THE AVADHUT

P.O. Box 8080
Santa Cruz, CA 95816
(408) 425-3531

A spritual community with the wise and compassionate guidance of the Self-Realized sage Nome. Meditation and open dialogue with Nome is available to all sincere seekers of Enlightenment. Call or write for introductory information.

BRIGID COLLECTIVE

2012 10th Street
Berkeley, CA 94710

Brigid is a collectively-owned home in Berkeley, begun in February, 1985. There are six owner-residents and one nine year old boy in our spacious duplex. Our house is three stories, with three baths, separate bedrooms, an assortment of common space and a large yard. Occasionally we have openings for new owner-residents.

Our agreements include a weekly dinner and meeting, quarterly retreats, regular upkeep of our home, sharing food, but more important, clear communication and consensus process. We value emotional sharing and are supportive of each other's growth. We are a combination of ritualists and meditators, environmentalists and feminists,and are involved in healing ourselves. We value our friends outside the house, our families and our work. We strive to give our nine-year-old artist his space, some continuity and our listening side.

Contact us by writing first to Brigid Collective.

"There is an increasing concern for the humanization of organizations, an increasing desire by people to feel more connected with each other, to act on their own environment rather than feeling acted upon."
--Vladimir Dupre

CAMPBELL HOT SPRINGS/ CONSCIOUSNESS VILLAGE

1 Campbell Hot Springs Rd. Box 234
Sierraville, CA 96126
(916) 994-8984 or 994-3677

Campbell Hot Springs/Consciousness Village is a small community living on 680 acres of mountainside and meadow 5000 feet up in Northern California.

We use simple practices to clean and balance the energy body with the help of earth, air, fire, water, spiritual family and thought-awareness.

We are an international training center for rebirthing/conscious breathing and spiritual purification and run week-long trainings every week plus some weekend events and longer trainings. Write or phone for our current rates and more information. We offer facilities for vision quests.

CENTER FOR THE EXAMINED LIFE (formerly Center for Psychological Revolution)

1525 Hornblend St.
San Diego, CA 92109
(619) 273-4673

Former church buildings in beach community.

"Group" of seven members (involved 16-21 years.) seeking to completely straighten out their lives, relations with each other, as basis for new approach to psychology, society.

Members started with serious emotional problems, including autism. Philosophy based on "mental structure and process" and "interpersonal justice" under the guidance of visionary leader, Constance Lerner Russell.

Two administrative members live at the Center, others nearby. Seven residential spaces are available for principled, serious individuals not practicing this philosophy. Exchange work-hours for rooms; minimum three month commitment. Send SASE for brochure, or $2.00 for literature.

COMMUNITY EVOLVING

P. O. Box 2481
Grass Valley, CA 95945
(916) 273-6706

Who are we? On the surface, we are Janie, DiAnne, Craig, Peter, Cory and Maurice sharing a home in Grass Valley. We place much value on raising our children and ourselves in a healthy emotional environment. We are looking for more people to join our household, and for more households to form, creating a broader, land-based community. We are moving onto a lovely 50-acre piece of land early this summer.

At present, we gather several times a week without the children for business and emotion-sharing meetings, and weekly for a family meeting where children participate fully. All our decisions are made by consensus. In our daily lives we like to experiment with various structures gleaned from many sources.

We envision the creation of a tribal village consisting of several extended families clustered on the land. Each group household would form around affinities on issues of lifestyle, personal chemistry, and areas of interest. Households will come together forming a tribal council where broader, community-wide issues will be discussed and decided.

Underlying all this is the desire to be deeply involved in each others' lives, to be sources of inspiration and learning for each other, and to grow older and wiser together.

COMMUNITY PLAN-IT
c/o Peace Theological Seminary
3500 W. Adams Blvd.
Los Angeles, CA 90018

Community Plan-It has as its goal the transformation of the planet. We are designing a planned cooperative community that enables us to live in greater harmony and balance with ourselves, each other, and our environment. In this community, it is necessary that our lifestyle not only has abundance and success, but is also nurturing and fun. In creating such a model community, others will be able to see how we can all cooperate and enjoy a higher standard of living. Eventually, we envision that the replication of our community or similar models will have a transforming effect on individual and world peace and the prosperity of all mankind. Currently, we are in the process of locating land and securing the funding to build the initial community of up to 500 people.

We consider issues such as how to incorporate the latest technology and how to live in harmony with nature to be very important. However, our primary concern is how we interact and relate with one another and how we make decisions that include and involve everyone--a process we call consensus. Through the Peace Theological Seminary, we have been having classes on how to work consensus while we continue the steps towards creating Community Plan-It.

COMPTCHE COMMUNITY FARMS
920 St. Helena Avenue
Santa Rosa, CA 95404
(707) 546-3809
Contact: Russ Neuman

Comptche Community Farms, Inc. was formed for the purpose of establishing a rural, residential community with two major aims: to create a loving and supportive living environment for ourselves and our children in which we can grow and learn freely together and to foster the art of living close to the land, serving as conscious, respectful stewards of the natural world around us, and directly experiencing the bonds which connect us to the earth and all its various forms of life. We see these aims as necessarily intertwined, each enhancing the other, and both together expressing our best vision of a responsible and joyful way of life.

We are now looking for at least two other families with a commitment to creating a supportive and cooperative lifestyle in a shared rural farm community, and who are also financially responsible and capable of fulfilling our financial requirements.

What members receive is the opportunity to participate in creating a real community, and to learn with the rest of us how to live life in a very different (and, we believe, a healthier and happier) way than our general urban society has taught us.

The property is located 12 miles from the costal town of Mendocino, California. There are two year-round creeks. Excellent soil for organic farming and many good building sites where families may build their own homes.

THE DOLPHIN TRIBE
1425 W. 221 St.
Torrance, CA 90501

Founded in 1979 in Human society, the Dolphin Tribe is the Human face of an ancient Dolphin spiritual culture which predates Human evolution by over 50 million years. We have land in the tropical Pacific with food trees and water. We will live a native lifestyle, in harmony with the ecosystem propagating indigenous food trees and traveling in outrigger canoes. The Dolphin Tribe is a church whose purposes include the return of Earth to Nature and Humans to Godhood through integration with transcendental dolphin and whale cultures, the use of transcendental technology and transcendental love. We practice Dolphin Shamanism and apprentice to dolphin master shamans through out-of-body traveling and shape-shifting to Dolphin form. We hope to have at least 10 permanent community members by the summer of 1989. There is no cost, but new members should plan on self support through cottage industries. Community income will be from ship building, video tapes and books. Members can swim with dolphins, communicate with them through music, meditation and play. Other activities will include hot tubbing, ritual majik, building undersea habitats, making friends with dolphins, whales, elephants, apes and extraterrestrials.

EXPANDING LIGHT ANANDA GUEST PROGRAMS
14618 Tyler Foot Rd.
Nevada City, CA 95959
(800) 346-5350

One of the world's most successful spiritual communities. We offer programs in meditation, hatha yoga, spiritualizing daily life and much more.

GLEN IVY
25000 Glen Ivy Road
Corona, CA 91719
(714)735-8701

Glen Ivy (est. 1977) is the Southwest regional center of the Emissaries of Divine Light. It is a spiritual education community where people may come for an experience of the Art of Living. Communal living is not an end in itself for the Emissaries, but is used to create a still environment that makes it easy for an individual to have a greater experience of his or her true identity. The permanent residents are charged with the task of putting this expansive spirit into practice in everyday duties and relationships. Such harmonization with the currents of life are seen as essential for personal, as well as global fulfillment.

Approximately 85 people of all ages make Glen Ivy their home. We invite you to come visit on Sunday and share in our morning radiation service (10:30 a.m.). If you find yourself resonating with the values outlined above, we encourage you to attend a one or five-day Art of Living seminar. Address all correspondence to Bob Kauffman.

HARBIN HOT SPRINGS
P.O. Box 782
Middletown, CA 95461
(707) 987-2477

Harbin Hot Springs is a clothing-optional, 1,100-acre New Age community/teaching center nestled in a quiet valley with clean air and pure spring water. We

have been in existence since 1972 and have well over 100 adult members who operate, maintain and improve a hot springs retreat and conference facility. There are many challenging opportunities here for those skilled in construction, mechanics, carpentry housekeeping, healing, administration, computing, etc.

If you are interested in applying for residency, or wish to consider establishing a program of your own here, your inquiry is invited. Financial assistance for projects is sometimes available. We are a smoke-free community. Use of drugs, alcohol or tobacco is not permitted.

There are many important details concerning visiting, meals, workshops, pets, children and residency that are not covered in this listing, so we recommend calling or writing (Attn: Community Relations) before visiting us. Please enclose $1 for postage.

HOW TO GET HERE: Take Highway 29 north from the Napa Valley to Middletown, Turn left (west) at the Union 76 gas station; then right at the stop sign and continue four miles, keeping left at the fork in the road. Open 24 hours a day, 365 days a year. (See "Articles" section.)

HEARTWOOD INSTITUTE, LTD.
220 Harmony Lane
Garberville, CA 95440
(707) 923-2021

Est. 1978. Heartwood Institute is a teaching community of dedicated, concerned people. We are concerned about how men and women can live in balance with our Mother Earth. We are concerned about the quality of our experience with each other.

Our mission is to provide resources for attaining higher physical, psychological and spiritual well-being. Our intent is to act as a catalyst for planetary healing through personal transformation. This is accomplished through programs of study, workshops and wellness retreats offered to both professionals and the general public.

Our nine-month residential certification programs are the foundation of our reputation as a center for professional training in the Natural Healing Arts. They are unique because they take place in an environment of professional excellence, support for personal unfoldment and the inspiring natural beauty of the Northern California Wilderness. One and two-week intensives are also offered throughout the year for certification, career enhancement and personal transformation.

Invitations are extended each quarter to a limited number of individuals to experience Heartwood Institute by participating in the Work Exchange Program. This program is intended as an experience in the total life of the Heartwood Community. It is a work-oriented program both physically and emotionally. You commit 28 hours per week of work assignment based on the needs of the community. In exchange, participants receive meals and may use Heartwood facilities. Write for application.

KERISTA COMMUNE
543 Frederick St.
San Francisco, CA 94117
(415) 753-1314

Urban-based, democratic, egalitarian community into polyfidelity (non-monogamy within fidelitous clusters of best friends), Macintosh computers, Utopian future vision and rock 'n roll. We use an intensive self-development and interpersonal communication process (Gestalt-O-Rama) to promote personal growth and clean relationships. We are fun-loving, intellectual, and interested in helping to solve global problems. Established in 1971; we are currently 26 adult members with three kids, and are now into voluntary childlessness (i.e., will not be producing any more kids ourselves). We operate a successful computer/graphics business, and publish The *Node* and *RockHEAD*. Seeking new members of like mind. Free illustrated handbook available.

L. A. CO-OPS &
THE SHARED HOUSING NETWORKER
P. O. Box 27731
Los Angeles, CA 90027
(213) 738-1254

Newsletter for those in the L.A. area interested in cooperatives and community/shared housing lifestyles.

Published every 8 weeks by CRSP, a public benefit, tax-exempt corporation committed to education and training for development of cooperatives of all kinds, and the Los Angeles Mutual Housing Association (LAMHA), a public benefit, tax-exempt corporation committed to cooperative housing and business development.

Send an SASE for sample newsletter.

THE MARIPOSA GROUP
501 W. Mariposa
El Segundo, CA 90245

A Conscious Community, we are creating an environment which promotes more joyful and fulfilling conditions for work, play and personal relationships. Our emphasis is on fully utilizing the emotional support, personal skills, education, financial resources and group energy available to us in a community such that each of us may achieve our fullest human potential. We are actively seeking new members who are willing to commit to making themselves, and this community, all that they can be. Children are welcome.

MARIPOSA SCHOOL
P. O. Box 387
Ukiah, CA 95482
(707) 462-1016

Community of nine adults and two children on 61 mostly wooded acres, 2-1/2 hours north of San Francisco, CA. We see ourselves as a family committed to caring for each other and sharing emotionally and economically. The major part of our income is derived from our alternative elementary school, and most of the rest is from a small sprout business. Through our teaching and other involvements, we commit ourselves to working toward a more equitable and ecological non-violent world.

We occasionally have openings for new members, so feel free to inquire.

NEW HRSIKESA FOUNDATION, INC.
Rt. 175, Box 469
Hopland, CA 95449

Kailas Mountain Community was established by Hansadutta Swami in 1978. Member of the Hare Krishna World Community. Located in the Mayacamas Mountain Range of Northern California, Mendocino County, on a valley farm. 30-40 members. Activities: Agriculture, construction, temple activities, etc. Followers of Bhakti Yoga as established by Lord Caitanya Mahaprabhu. Have four basic regulative principles of religious life: no meat-eating, no illicit sex, intoxication or gambling. Open to visitors and new members.

In the White man's society it seems that everybody is out for himself. White men have forgotten their responsibility to the community. They ignore the brotherhood of all mankind. Stalking Wolf taught me that I lived for myself when I lived for the tribe." --Tom Brown, Jr.

NEW MOON HOUSE
1516 Guerrero St.
San Francisco, CA 94110

Established 1983. House of communication and child-raising. We live on a noisy city street and come together for dinner every night, sharing our city adventures. Presently 10 adults, two children, wood shop, library, free store and organic backyard garden. We are TV-free, mostly vegetarian and non-smoking. Very interested in knowing and communicating with other communities. Please write first if you would like to visit.

THE OJAI FOUNDATION
P. O. Box 1620
Ojai, CA 93023
(805) 646-8343

The Ojai Foundation is a non-sectarian, educational and environmentally concerned non-profit organization. It is a place where new ideas can be explored and realized with many retreat leaders from different cultures and disciplines. We have a work-scholar program at the cost of $375 per month. We welcome people with skills in gardening, carpentry, cooking, public relations, office administration, and basic land and living. Write for further info. (See "Articles" section.)

OUR LAND COOPERATING COMMUNITY
P. O. Box 185
El Nido, CA 95317

No Religious preference. Area--Central Valley, CA. A proposed modern Kibbutz-type cooperating community based on high ideals and sound economics. It is to be comprised of the management, organizers and activists dedicated to making it more rewarding financially, environmentally, culturally and socially to be more human than inhuman, to build and live the dream. We have 2,300 acres of beautiful farmland and are organizing in the owner-operator area of commodity processing and distribution.

PACHA MAMA
1067 Main St.
Susanville, CA 96130

Pacha Mama (Mother Earth). We are starting a cooperative community and we are looking for a few exceptional members: mentally mature, good at heart, spiritual, non-drinkers, non-smokers. We have a wonderful bed and breakfast in Susanville, CA, and

we plan to imitate the Ananda system. Former nuns, priests and Ananda members are more than welcome. We need leaders and good people eager to live a better life looking together for love, peace, happiness and prosperity. Please write to: Alberto Bucar, 3415 Woodside Rd., Woodside, CA 94062, or after 5 p.m. call (415) 851-0902.

ROANDOAK OF GOD CHRISTIAN COMMUNE
Attn: Zonah Baruth
455A Chorro Creek Rd.
Morro Bay, CA 93442
(805) 772-9985

Like the early church, Roandoak of God lives, works, worships, and reaches out to others as one big happy family. Combining work programs and church programs, our 15 year old community has helped hundreds overcome even great problems. Nearly 1,000 arrive each year. No one turned away. Many referred by probation, hotline, churches, etc. Mainly self-supporting. Population 110 to 150. All ages and backgrounds. Serving the Lord, living by the Bible. It is very full and rewarding to live here.

RUSSELLS MILLS
c/o David & Darice Lei
P.O. Box 75
Murphy's, CA 95247
(209) 728-3504

Russells Mills is a new community on an established farm. Now six members. Christians with loving and sharing feelings. Have goats, chickens, rabbits, bees, apple orchard, blackberries, haying land and equipment and large garden. 86 acres of rolling hills, five miles from the nearest small town. Looking for singles and couples with or without children to help make the community a self-sustaining community. Also have auto shop, cabinet shop, and other small businesses you could join. This is Murphy's, CA, in the Mother Lode Mountains.

SANTA ROSA CREEK COMMONS
887 Sonoma Ave. #3
Santa Rosa, CA 95404
(707) 523-0626 or (707) 527-7191

A limited equity housing cooperative for all ages; 50 miles north of San Francisco; has 27 units (studio to three bedroom), community room, laundry facilities, wooded area on the creek at the rear of its two acres; near central Santa Rosa. Members serve on committees and are responsible for managing and maintaining the property. Ten units are for low-income people. Membership shares purchased at time of occupancy based on the size of unit occupied (assisted $680-$2080; others $5800-$10,800). Monthly carrying charges are pro-rated to meet expenses. Applications are being received for future occupancy.

SIERRA HOT SPRINGS
P.O. Box 366
Sierraville, CA 96126
(916) 994-3773

New Age Spiritual Community forming at rural hot springs in Sierra Mountains. Work in exchange for rent; 14 hours of work per week for a room or 10 hours of work per week for camping. Skilled and unskilled workers needed. No drug use, smoking or intoxication permitted. Call or write for more information.

"It has consistently been found that for maximum effect experiences designed to foster such sensory awakening should be shared experiences. Not only is it more fun to have these experiences in a small, congenial group, but individual growth and change appear to be more intense and lasting."--Herbert A. Otto

STARCROSS MONASTERY
P. O. Box 14279
Santa Rosa, CA 95404

Progressive Catholic community of men/women. Ministry to children with AIDS.

UNIVERSITY OF THE TREES
P. O. Box 644
Boulder Creek, CA 95006

The University of the Trees is an intense, fast growth environment for self-realization. The community uses three main methods of working on the ego: selfless service, Creative Conflict and meditation. Creative Conflict is a method of deep bonding communication developed by the community's founder, Christopher Hills. The community has been going on for 17 years. Part of its vision is to build a healing temple. Another vision is a world freed from hunger through the spread of the nutritious Spirulina plankton.

ZEN CENTER OF LOS ANGELES
923 S. Normandie Ave.
Los Angeles, CA 90006
(213) 387-2351

ZCLA was established in 1967 under the direction of Taizan Maezumi Roshi. Maezumi Roshi has lived in the United States for the past 32 years. He has received Dharma transmission through both Soto and Rinzai lines. His formal training and life experience has made him uniquely qualified to teach western students. Roshi's senior students have established centers throughout the western world.

ZCLA now has two locations offering year-round training. The city center, which is located in the heart of the Wilshire District, offers residents the unique opportunity for maximum participation in a daily zazen schedule, with monthly retreats, while still maintaining a secular life of family and outside work. Positions are also available for those who want to participate as full-time trainees. Morning and evening sitting is open to the public. Thursday evening talks given by Roshi and senior students are also open. The city center offers the serious student of Zen a close, supportive community of both laymen and monks. City center's location is central to major universities, theaters, and museums. Public transportation is readily available.

Our Zen Mountain Center has just recently begun offering a year-round residential training program. This secluded and beautiful setting of pine, cedar, and oak trees is located in the San Jacinto Mountains, 120 miles east of Los Angeles. Mountain center is now quite civilized, offering a variety of classes and special retreats. The 90-day summer training program is truly an international event, attracting students from Japan, Europe, Canada, and Mexico. Those who are interested in this training program should apply early as there are a limited number of openings.

For further information, please contact us.

ZENDIK FARM

1431 Tierra del Sol Road
Boulevard, CA 92005
(619) 766-4095

We are a communal tribe living on a 75-acre farm about 90 miles east of San Diego, not too far from the Mexican border, along the Tecate Divide. Mechanics, carpentry, homeschooling, muzik, graphix, animal husbandry, organic gardening. We have a psycho/punk band and publish a quarterly environmental arts underground magazine, circulation 15,000, copies available on request. We have started a political party called Z.A.P. (Zendik Action Party-- membership as of March '89=1500), the main objective of which is to get mostly young people working together to throw out the old society and build a new one. Call or write for further information.

COLORADO

HOOKER HOUSE

3151 W. 24th Ave.
Denver, CO 80211
(303) 477-5176

Twelve-year-old middle-class cooperative. We live in a 100 year old home which is owned by two members. Only philosophy is that cooperative living is practical and comfortable. All members have outside jobs and share household expenses. All accumulate equity in the house, which is returned if they leave. Allow smoking, T.V., cars, junk food and enjoy affluent middle-class lifestyle. House accounts are balanced with one member's micro-computer.

STILLPOINT

Rye Star Route
Wetmore, CO 81253
(303) 784-6194

Gia-Fu Feng was born in Shanghai in 1919, came to U. S. in 1947 to study Comparative Culture. In the early 60's he helped start the Esalen Institute. His books include *Tao Te Ching, Chuang Tse, I Ching*, etc. In Stillpoint you follow a simple diet and a precise daily schedule. Learning through apprenticeship and observing nature. Gia-Fu Feng teaches Taoist meditation to achieve inner tranquility to participate in the cosmic process.

SUNRISE RANCH COMMUNITY

5569 N. County Rd. 29
Loveland, CO 80537

Headquarters of Emissary Foundation International. 140 permanent residents in '88. On 350 acres, dedicated to revealing the practical application of spiritual values in everyday life.

Conducts numerous seminars, hosts conferences for diverse disciplines/professions concerned with world condition. Members live in apartments/private homes, most meals taken together. Children go to local schools. Occupations vary: farming, construction, gardening, animals, carpentry/machine shops, office work, writing, editing, drawing, photographing, printing, kitchen help, child care, painting, weeding, canning, maintaining beauty throughout the ranch. Dynamic/well-organized community. Over 200 centers similar throughout globe.

TRUTH CONSCIOUSNESS
SACRED MOUNTAIN ASHRAM

3305 County Road 96
Ward, CO 80481-9606.
(303) 447-1637 or 444-4027

The purpose of life or creation is to grow consciously toward the Divine, our source--as the flower unfolding its beauty to the sun. In keeping with these words of Swami Amar Jyoti, Truth Consciousness was founded in 1974 and presently maintains ashrams in Ward (CO), Tucson (AZ), and Rockford (MI), as well as Community Centers in Boulder and Tucson. These centers provide a setting for devotees and disciples to grow spiritually under the direct guidance of the Master. Weekly Satsangs (Spiritual Discourse), meditation, yoga instruction, and retreats held throughout the year are open to all sincere seekers. (See "Articles" section.)

DISTRICT OF COLUMBIA

3HO FOUNDATION
1704 Q St., N.W.
Washington, D.C. 20009
(202) 483-6660

80 adults, 30 children living in ashrams near Dupont Circle. As a daily discipline, all practice Yoga and meditation before dawn, most are practicing members of the Sikh faith. Monogamous marriage is encouraged. Average age is 29 years old, children are from newborn to age 12. Own and operate many successful businesses in D.C., including Golden Temple Restaurant and Shakti Shoes. Emphasis is on service in the surrounding D.C. community. Offer classes in Yoga, meditation, natural food cooking and natural healing techniques.

COMMUNITY FOR CREATIVE NON-VIOLENCE
425 Second Street, NW
Washington, D.C. 20001
(202) 393-1909

CCNV is a religous community of service and resistance located in downtown Washington, DC. We began in late 1970 as an expression of faith and moral outrage to the war in Vietnam. Since 1976, CCNV has worked predominantly with domestic poverty issues. Currently we provide food, shelter, clothing and medical care to 1,200 homeless people each day. We feed hungry people--and ourselves--with discarded and surplus food; we clothe homeless people--and ourselves--with the excess of others. No one in CCNV receives a salary. Over half of the community members are formerly homeless. We are non-hierarchical in structure and decisions are made consensually.

We welcome inquiries from people who are interested in being part of CCNV's work. We can provide you with the necessary further information.

FLORIDA

FLORIDA GROUP RETREAT
P. O. Box 2133
Leesburg, FL 32748

Functioning survivalist community in Florida. Beautiful property with controlled lake access. Secure but convenient. Flexibility of using standard housing, mobile homes or recreational vehicles. Ideally suited for permanent or weekend use as well as a safe haven. Replies strictly confidential. Reply to F.G.R., address above.

THE HEART
P. O. Box 1211
De Leon Springs, FL 32028

'The Heart' is a small family of gentle beings following the path of consciousness. We live on 12-1/2 acres of wooded rolling hills amid large Oak and Pine trees. The Angel of the Waters is present on the large private lake which adjoins our sanctuary.

We love and respect all of the many paths to the Divine, and find our deepest teachings coming from the simple life of committed relationship and familyhood. Children are our major focus, we home birth, we home school, and have developed a gender-balanced way of relating to the Universe. We welcome the Rising Star of the Feminine aspect of the Great Spirit now being born into earth consciousness. The Divine Mother is our lover.

We are Vegetarians, we offer love and protection to all living beings in our domain, we are learning about self sufficiency and reliance, and we are studying the Arts as our form of right livelihood. Music, organic gardening, and Native American Teachings go together in our circles. Radha Krishnas' pure transcendental love is fragrant in the air.

Wintertime travellers are welcome to camp or park their live-in vehicles in our space in exchange for $5.00 per night or a mutually agreeable energy exchange. Artist and crafts folk have been coming here for years now to do the many fine Wintertime Art Festivals throughout Florida. We are centrally located, non-commercial, and we don't think nude is crude. We ask all that come here to respect our conventions, no meat eating, no intoxication, no weapons.

Possible full time living situation for any sister or brother who can show their love and gentleness and sincerity. An in-depth letter and photo of yourself will receive immediate response anytime but the Rainbow month. Photos of artwork or skills especially welcome, we will consider every aspect.

"But I say to you that when you work you fulfill a part of earth's furthest dream, assigned to you when that dream was born...And when you work with love you bind yourself to yourself, and to one another, and to God."--The Prophet

GEORGIA

JUBILEE PARTNERS

P. O. Box 68
Comer, GA 30629
(404)783-5131

Jubilee Partners is a Christian service community, our main work being to serve as an orientation center for refugees. Our orientation program includes 18 hours of English classes per week for about eight weeks, in addition to other types of orientation such as field trips, shopping in supermarkets, driving and nutrition classes, etc. Refugees who have been through our program leave here and go to sponsoring families or groups. In the past we have had Cuban, Vietnamese, Cambodian and Laotian people with us, and at present we have refugees from El Salvador here.

Part of our staff here is permanent, and part of it is made up of volunteers who come here for periods of from three to five months. Since we are a Christian community, we prefer that volunteers who come here be Christian also.

KOINONIA PARTNERS

Rt. 2
Americus, GA 31709
(912)924-0391

Koinonia, started in 1942, is a service-oriented community located on a farm near Plains, Georgia, that seeks to be faithful to Jesus Christ and the Kingdom of God. A house building program that began in 1969 is vigorous--by the end of '88, 170 new houses had been made available to low income people, at cost and with no-interest mortages. We have an extensive educational ministry, and are active in peace witnessing, prison visitation, etc. We support ourselves by farming and a mail order business. New members are welcome; the membership process begins by coming for three months as part of a volunteer group--write or visit for more information.

HAWAII

KAHUMANA FARM AND COMMUNITY

86-660 Lualualei Hmstd. Rd.
Waianae, HI 96792
Devoted to healing the major crippling disease of our time--mental and emotional illness. We at Kahumana Special Treatment Facility share our daily lives with 12 "Special Residents" at our home, a 14-acre farm. Work includes the Kahumana Counseling Center which serves over 100 local psychiatric out-patients monthly. Healing human relationships is an on-going process for the core group of the community. Together we represent a wide range of social, cultural and religious backgrounds. We seek to cultivate a common heart and all-embracing love which transcends the limits of sex, race, creed, profession. Each has freely chosen to make a commitment to reach for Accordance (unity in diversity) to help wounded souls.

MOTHER EARTH CHURCH OF OPIHIHALE

P. O. Box 172
Honaunau, HI 96726
Attn: Rev. Luke Aitken

Cooperative community of seven adults, four children. Farm/multi-adult extended family/social experiment living under fairly primitive conditions (no electricity, phone, rain water, catchment, plastic trap roofs) on nine acres of rain forest 20 miles from town. Diet mostly vegetarian, evolving toward eating what we grow and trade for. Farm design is permaculture/integrated agriculture model.

Planning orchards, gardens, building a community kitchen. Families are independent, self-reliant people who prefer the economics/emotional satisfaction of interdependence. Individual sleep houses, shared kitchen. Cooking, food buying, etc. done cooperatively. Eventually will make the land available for New Age workshops and spiritual healing retreats. Open to visitors on short-term, limited work exchange basis.

OHANA MAUKA

P.O. Box 9
c/o Russ Down, M.D.
Pahala, HI 96777
(808) 928-8019 or
(609) 465-4878 (N.J.)

Half mile high & six from ocean, at center backwall of Wood Valley, is an outback 35-acre oasis for sustainable diversified eco-ag, ringed by National Forest, cane monoculture & ranchland. Attractions: developed gardens, plenty of bananas, common kitchen, ocean view, Tibetan Temple for neighbor. Needs: kindred spirit literate outdoor worker types, familiar with tropical plants, orchards,grafting, jury-rigging, permaculture, land trusts, polyfidelity/other nontraditional family, "Earth First," etc., but willing to often weed-eat/mow 'til dark, then "talk story."

ILLINOIS

PLOW CREEK FELLOWSHIP
Rt. 2, Box 2A
Tiskilwa, IL 61368
(815) 646-4249

Plow Creek Fellowship, founded in 1971, is a Christian communal church located on a 189-acre farm near Tiskilwa, Illinois, with a part of the group located in the village of Tiskilwa.

There are 30+ adult members ranging in age from early 30's to early 60's and over 35 children. Fellowship life is supported by a number of Fellowship-owned businesses and by some members who work at jobs outside the Fellowship.

The Fellowship is affiliated with the Mennonite church. Members make a commitment to Jesus as Lord, discipleship, pacifism, fidelity in marriage and chastity outside of marriage, mutual decision-making, and a communal economic life.

The Fellowship welcomes guests and those considering joining our life together. We are open to new members and to children. To visit or obtain more information write or phone Richard Foss at (815) 646-4264.

STELLE
Box 123
Stelle, IL 60919

Building a "model city" where all the many different resources for personal and social transformation will be available in a mutually supportive environment. Established in 1973 upon *The Ultimate Frontier*, Stelle presently consists of 125 residences, 44 homes, 240 acres, a factory, businesses, schools, food co-op, greenhouses, and holistic health center, individual homes, employment, diet and religious/philosophical beliefs. Innovative educational programs emphasizing early learning and parental participation. Individuals accept personal responsibility for self-development and govern ourselves through a participatory democracy. Achieving self-sufficiency through R & D with technology and cooperative linkages with neighbors. Home of *Communities, Journal of Cooperation* and the Fellowship of Intentional Communities.

VIVEKANANDA VEDANTA SOCIETY
5423 S. Hyde Park Blvd.
Chicago, IL 60615
(312) 363-0027

A branch of the Ramakrishna Math and Mission, which was founded by Swami Vivekananda with the twin ideals of realizing God through spiritual practices and living your life for the welfare of all beings. The Vivekananda Vedanta Society has a Temple in Chicago, and a rural ashram in Ganges, Michigan. Both centers give regular classes and have libraries and book shops.

INDIANA

OAKWOOD
R.R. 1, Box 659
Selma, IN 47383
(317) 282-0484

Est. 1973, 30 people, all ages, on 326 acres of hardwood trees, prime Indiana farmland, organic farming, some animal husbandry and a small orchard. Setting for weekend and one-week Spiritual Leadership seminars. Owned and operated by Emissary Foundation International, a not-for-profit corporation dedicated to the regeneration of mankind through the accurate handling of everyday circumstances.

PADANARAM SETTLEMENT/ GOD'S VALLEY
Box 478, R.R. 1
Williams, IN 47435
(812) 388-5571

Padanaram Settlement was established in 1966 as a utopian, idealistic society. Its 200 members are employed in one of the businesses (sawmilling, log cabins, bark mulch, trucking) or in kitchenwork, bakery, gardening, cannery, the schools (nursery, preschool, elementary or high), carpentry, or construction. It is dedicated to equal educaton, philosophical analysis, social idealism, economic independence, and religious non-denominationalism.

Meals are served at a common table three times daily. Dramas, poetry, mime, music, and dancing on special occasions. Hiking, boatin, hunting, fishing, swimming, horseback riding on the land. The nuclear family is retained within the larger extended family.

There are two conventions per year, spring, and fall (usually May and October). Padanaram Settlement is becoming a dynamic force in providing an open forum for discussion on philosophy, religion, politics, ecology, education, economics, and social life having to do with a worldwide network of cooperative communities called the International Communal Utopia (ICU).

An Open House is held mid October for the surrounding communities. For more information write to: Rachel Summerton.

KANSAS

AURORA MENDIA, RAY ANDERSON
P. O. Box 20341
Wichita, KS 67208
(316)686-7100

Two of us are trying to find other people in Kansas or surrounding states who would like to get together for a couple of days to check each other out as to our compatibility for living and working together in a small (five - seven member), leaderless, urban group. The central purpose of the group is to do everything we can to bring about an alternative social order, one giving top priority to the process that generates ever new levels and dimensions of mutual understanding and appreciation. The group will feature direct communication, giving and receiving feedback, no-lose conflict resolution, and openness to new possibilities of constructive action. Please phone or write if you would like to join us in a mutual check-out.

SUNFLOWER HOUSE
1406 Tennessee St.
Lawrence, KS 66044
(913) 749-0871 or 841-0484

Sunflower House is a cooperative for students at the University of Kansas. The co-op is open to all students, regardless of race, color or creed. Our community is based on the book *Walden II*, by B. F. Skinner. Members receive credits for doing work, which they can exchange for reductions in rent.

Sunflower House is affiliated with a group of researchers at the University of Kansas, who are studying procedures for promoting harmonious group living. They hope to develop a model that can be used to start other small cooperatives.

Y.C.C. COMMUNITIES
2843 Keywest Ct.
Wichita, KS 67204

Dynamic growing spiritual society, over 200 communities. Primary goal: Self-Realization, specializing in meditation as propounded by Vyasa (author of *Vedas*). Management: President. Income: communal effort, various forms. Members: men, women, children, dedicated to developing love of God (Krishna). Vegetarian communal meals, ancient Vedic ceremonies, private schools sometimes available with a strong spiritual orientation, Sunday Love Feasts, transcendental music offering personal involvement (bhajana's/kirtana's), family/single lifestyles, visiting facilities. Guest requirements: rise before dawn, attend meditation program, some work, follow four Yoga principles, no meat eating, gambling, intoxication, illicit sex. Everything centers around God consciousness, specializing in Bhakta Yoga. A community for serious seekers. (Home study Yoga Course for the less communal-minded.) Present address NOT a community--for purpose of connection only. Write for information and full listing.

KENTUCKY

FUTURES
111Bobolink
Berea, KY 40403
(606) 986-8000

(See "Articles" section)

SPIRAL
P. O. Box 337
Monticello, KY 42633

Spiraland is 250 acres in the foothills of southcentral Kentucky. Spiral is legally a Land Trust and holds the land "in perpetuity" for present and future generations of wimmin. We are a Lesbian Feminist community but welcome all wimmin. Our community is based upon Permacultue (sustainable agriculture) principles. We believe the land is a self-sustaining ecological system of which we are a part. We are striving towards self-sufficiency, but are in the pioneering stages of that dream.

There are two houses on the land with others under construction. Community members are required to pay a nonrefundable Land Trust fee based on the number of community members living on, or intending to live on the land. Visitors welcome.

LOUISIANA

HOLY CITY COMMUNITY
Rt. 7, Box 390
Lake Charles, LA 70601
(318)855-2871

Est. 1970. Family-based community with a vision of an alternative society based on Gospel values. Live on 60 acres of swampy woodland, are financially self-supporting, try to maintain simple lifestyle. Fifteen nuclear families, two single people, clergy, religious and lay, young and old. Covenant community in the Roman Catholic tradition, subject to authority of Bishop and designated leadership. Life is centered in God: Father, Son and Holy Spirit, model of perfect community. Understand ourselves to be in God's image most fully as a community rather than as individual persons, and together we aspire to a life of Gospel poverty.

SUNEIDESIS CONSOCIATION VALAASHBY FARMS
P. O. Box 628
Burmas, LA 70041

Located on a beautiful island approximately 75 miles south of New Orleans. Has no membership per se, but is supported by 10 fellow residents and 15 contributing associates. Est. 1975, sponsors projects such as World Hunger Objectives, as well as other far-reaching planetary goals. Experimental society searching for alternative lifestyles, using all means to encourage the rise of the new Concomitant Intelligence through national lectures, rap sessions and workshops. There are also frequent gatherings and symposiums on the island, as well as weekend workshops, and a quarterly newsletter, *Touchpoint.* We are a world service group who would like to network with others whose concerns are for a more equitable and humane world order. Visitors are always welcome!

MAINE

S.E.A.D.S. OF TRUTH, INC.
262 Georgetown Rd.
Columbia
Harrington, ME 04643
(207) 483-9763

S.E.A.D.S. means Solar Energy Awareness and Demonstration Seminars.)

We are a fluid group of 6-12 persons with rotating responsibilities, working towards a Self-Sufficient community landtrust. On 60 wooded acres in rural/coastal Washington Co., Maine (Sunrise County) we operate an maintain and "on-going, hands-on" seminar center developing do-it-yourself solar projects. During the past nine years we have travelled around the country giving workshops and helping others towards a self-sufficient lifestyle.

We are open year round for short and long-term visitors and are actively seeking families and individuals interested in participating directly or through supportive membership. We would like to share our experience and look forward to your communications. (See "Articles" section.)

MARYLAND

HEATHCOTE CENTER
21300 Heathcote Rd.
Freedom, MD 21053
(301) 592-9013

Women's community/retreat/conference center, 30 miles from Baltimore. 35 acres, woods/meadows in a land trust, we're buying the buildings. Organic gardening, renovating buildings. Conference center--we offer workshops, rent for group/individual retreats--hope to make this a cottage industry. Feminist perspective, collective process, support for political involvement, strong ties with Baltimore women's community. Looking for women with skills to join collective/staff; teach what they know--any building skills, on the land skills, healing arts, fund raising, organizing, creative arts. Long or short-term commitment; investment possibilities for non-residents.

WOODBURN HILL FARM
Route 3, Box 125
Mechanicsville, MD 20659
(301)884-5615

Rural adult-oriented community in Southern Maryland 40 miles from Washington, D.C. founded in 1975 on 120-acre former Amish farm. Now five adults and two teenagers in residence. Looking for members/renters.

Holistic health orientation, personal growth, organic gardening, common kitchen, separate and shared housing, privacy, New Games, parties, and celebration of various rituals. Diet tends toward vegetarian and includes poultry and seafood.

Governance by consensus. Finances are "cost-shared". Most adults work in education or health professions. Some are politically active. Are you interested in cottage industry? Organic farming? Call or write for info or to arrange your visit in advance.

MASSACHUSETTS

THE CENTER OF THE LIGHT
P. O. Box 540
Gt. Barrington, MA 01230
(413)229-2396

The Center Of The Light is an educational retreat center dedicated to the teaching and prospering of healing and spiritual growth. It is located on 78 acres in southwestern Massachusetts, in the Berkshire Mountains.

During the summer, from the end of May through September, the Center presents a full program of experiential workshops. Topics for 1989 include herbal studies, massage, facial rejuvenation, shiatsu, Jesus and healing, the gifts of the Holy Spirit, music and imagery, Native American medicine wheel, kayaking, singing Black American gospel music, A.C.O.A. and meditation renewal retreats, and workshops for personal transformation. Weekend concerts, presentations, and weekly worship and healing services take place throughout the summer.

During the summer the Center also welcomes guests who would rather not take a program but would like to vacation in a tranquil, spiritually oriented setting with natural foods, recreational facilities, and the nourishing atmosphere generated by the land's beauty and the supportive staff.

During the non-summer months, October through April, the Center offers a few weekend workshops open to the public. Ongoing programs include the **Training For Healers Program**, a comprehensive training program in spiritual and natural healing and personal growth; an **Herbal Apprenticeship Training** and certification in **Facial Rejuvenation** massage.

COYOTE AND MIRA HEALING GRACE SANCTUARY
Shelburne Falls, MA 01370
(413)635-9386

We are presently two folks with a vision of sharing our home and our quest with a few other kindred spirits devoted to practical Godliness, harmony and healing in all realms. Our place is 85 acres in a lovely riverbend in rural New England's Berkshire Mountains.

Our Vocation and Dream is to be **catalysts for changing the course of human history**--turning us away from social and planetary ruin. Our vision of how to achieve such a major shift involves a reweaving of the whole tapestry of our selfhood, both personal and collective.

Our welcome extends to you to be guests in our home if you: share our beliefs and goals, and are enthused about joining our activities and endeavors; want to be a helpmate or intern, or to seriously consider us as potential family and place to put down roots; call before you come (413) 625-9386, 9am - 7pm; think kids are the greatest, believe in shared parenting, and are a kid at heart; know how to set and honor limits and; and are skilled at being helpful and respectful of others.

Want to know more about the seed of healthy culture that we're evolving and nurturing? Send for your copy of Healing Grace Sanctuary...Your Ticket to Harmony in All Realms. Please be sure to include a hug and a prayer and a few words of good cheer. A business size self-addressed, stamped envelope would be appreciated. (Suggestions and any other donations are always appreciated, too.)

FRIENDS COMMUNITY
Lincoln St.
N. Easton, MA 02356
(617)238-7679

Friends Community, an intentional grouping of 56 condominium homes on 86 acres midway between Boston and Providence, started in '79 by the Society of Friends. Owners form an Association which seeks people of all ages and faiths who desire to live together cooperatively in peace and harmony. Homes are solar heated, plain in design, and grouped closely to encourage neighborliness. Prime interests are sharing, caring, gardening, and managing woodlands and woodstoves for conservation.

KRIPALU CENTER FOR YOGA AND HEALTH
Box 793, West St.
Lenox, MA 01240
(413) 637-3280

Kripalu Center for Yoga and Health is a dynamic residential community of 220 men, women and children who are living a wholistic lifestyle of daily exercise, balanced vegetarian diet and focused, joyous work. Our community offers training programs to people from all over the world in such diverse areas as holistic health, yoga and massage. A special tuition-free program called Spiritual Lifestyle Training allows people to work in our community for a three-month period where they receive an in-depth experience of conscious living.

A beautiful setting in the Berkshire Mountains, the inspiring teachings of Yogi Amrit Desai, our founder/director, a special supportive loving family, are what Kripalu is all about.

(See "Articles" section.)

THE RENAISSANCE COMMUNITY, INC.
P. O. Box 272
Turner Falls, MA 01376
(413)863-9711

Sixteen year-old community with living facilities at The 2001 Center, Main Road, Gill, MA, where they are developing a "self-sufficient" village on 80 acres of land. Current membership approximately 80 adults, 45 children. Businesses include carpentry, excavating, bus company, recording studio, assorted hand crafts and farming. Visitors fee $10 per night.

SIRIUS COMMUNITY
Baker Road
Shutesbury, MA 01072
(413)259-1251

As a community, we are committed to living in attunement with God and acting as custodians for our 86 acres of land.

We honor the inter-connectedness of all life and are learning to work in harmony with the forces of nature in our garden and forest to create a healing of the earth. We respect the presence of God within each person and work to deepen our spiritual path through meditation and listening to the feedback we get from daily life. Group living at Sirius often acts as a purifying fire, presenting many opportunities for releasing old patterns. Problems between people arise here as they do anywhere, but we use the experience to work on our personal growth. Each member is free to follow whatever spiritual disciplines are most inspirational and helpful to him/her.

Our purpose as a community is to be a center of Light, a place of hope and positive vision for the future, serving the spiritual growth of members and visitors and teaching our spiritual values through practical skills such as organic gardening, solar building, vegetarian cooking. We are serving as agents of change, building bridges to the mainstream society to create together a more peaceful, loving world. Call or write for free brochure and sample journal.

(See "Articles" section.)

MICHIGAN

CIRCLE PINES CENTER
8650 Mullen Rd.
Delton, MI 94046
(616) 623-5555

Circle Pines Center is a non-profit, educational and recreational cooperative located on 360 acres of meadows, forests and a lake in Southwestern Michigan. We operate a summer camp for families and children featuring non-competitive games, cooperative work projects, peace education, group-building activities, canoeing and swimming, nature studies and creative arts. Open year-round with Spring/Fall conference and seminar space and with a Winter Weekends cross-country skiing and natural healing program. We are an AYH hostel. Supported by fees for our services, gifts, contributions, dues and donated labor by our members and friends.

(See "Articles" section.)

LAKE VILLAGE
7943 S. 25th St.
Kalamazoo, MI 49001

Another day dawns at Lake Village, a 115-acre working farm commune on the outskirts of Kalamazoo, MI. Residents have adapted to social and economic changes by planting their feet in two worlds.

They embrace organic farming, but some commute to traditional jobs. They make decisions about the commune as a group, but some bought and built on additional land expanding the Commune to a total 325 acres. They grow some of their own food, but also shop at grocery stores on the outside.

And this is not a work-for-your-keep setup. Residents pay their share of money for private quarters and even are charged a monthly parking fee, while those working full time as farm hands earn varying amounts per hour.

The Farm includes a variety of animals including sheep, goats, hogs, cattle, chickens, ducks, pigeons, geese, rabbits, peacocks, horses, etc. raised for the survival of all and respected as community members. Its business includes day care and other human services. It teaches all forms of survival skills to those living on the land (who serve both as students and staff) as well as to persons from the larger community. Members are both physically and spiritually active within the greater Community regarding issues relating to the well-being of Mother Earth and all her children.

SKY WOODS COSYNEGAL
P.O Box 4176
Muskegon Heights, MI 49444

Community of eight people living near the shores of Lake Michigan. Community established 12 years ago. Dedicated to a rational and compassionate rebirth of community. Believe that participation in our own and others self creation is the highest of artistic forms. Have a home, farm of a few acres, wood and sewing industries, are producing some arts and crafts and are deeply into wind and solar energy, group sufficiency, and organic gardening and orcharding.

We have begun to experience the ecstasy of shared lives. We have seen the fear of change overwhelmed through mutual support. Community has been our spirit--our inherent vehicle to transcendence and perfectability. Our goal is to be an egalitarian community.

We will mail a statement of our beliefs and purposes and answer any questions. Drop us a note with address/phone number. Visitors welcome, arrange in advance.

WOMYN-ONLY COMMUNITIES AND LAND GROUPS

The following is a partial list based on 1989 information. *Lesbian Connection* Magazine compiles and periodically prints updated information. Send long SASE with all requests for information.

ADOBELAND
Rt. 9, Box 820
Tucson AZ 85743

DOE FARM
(WISCONSIN WOMYN'S LAND CO-OP)
Rt. 2, Box 42
Norwalk, WI 54648
(608) 269-5301

DRAGON
Rt.1, Box 395
Ava, MO 65608

HEATHCOTE CENTER
21300 Heathcote Rd.
Freeland, MD 21053
(301) 343-0280

OWL FARM
(OREGON WOMEN'S LAND TRUST)
P. O. Box 1692
Roseburg, OR 97470

PAGODA/CRONE'S NEST
207 Coastal Hwy.,
St. Augustine, FL 32084
(904) 824-2970

RAINBOW'S END
Rt. 3, Box 3645
Roseburg, OR 97470 (503) 673-7649

SUSAN B. ANTHONY
MEMORIAL UNREST HOME
13423 Howard Rd.
Millfield, OH 45761

WHO FARM, INC.
37010 Snuffin Rd.
Estacada, OR 97023 (503) 630-6728

WOMANSHARE
Box 681
Grants Pass, OR 97526

UPLAND HILLS

Ecological Awareness Center
2575 Indian Lake Road
Oxford, MI 48051
(313)693-1021

Upland Hills Center, an umbrella organization which unites Upland Hills Farm, Upland Hills School and Upland Hills Ecological Awareness Center, is a living synergism. Twelve people from the three organizations are working toward restructuring our organizations in order to further our work, align with other organizations and to make more efficient use of our resources. After a careful examination of our respective current realities there emerged the following Vision and Mission Statements. There is a shared sense that we are all on the threshold of something very important.

The Upland Hills Center is a commitment to life-long experiences that recognize the unique gift in all individuals to make a difference. The Center provides opportunities for people to experience those human qualities that are common to all individuals so as to empower them to participate in the process of healing our planet.

To design, fund and facilitate programs that: promote global understanding through individual experiences and community outreach; provide people with opportunities to interact with nature and the farm; produce expressions of our vision to the global community through the media; be what we teach; and encourage synergism between organizations.

WELLNESS HOUSE

c/o David Wyannt
3586 W. Arbutus
Okemos, MI 48864

Wellness House: A Sanctuary for Radiant Being. Cooperative living in a healing context. To serve, teach, learn and grow in unconditional love, in a wholistic setting. Teaching rebirthing, Yoga, massage and hypnosis (with sauna and fireplace). Vegetarian potlucks every Sunday from 2:00 - 5:00 p.m. with Medicine Drum Ceremony, nature walks, weekend wellness intensives each month.

"Gifted with the genius to create ideas, we can meet old material needs with a new urge - an urge to preserve what we cannot replace. Wilderness made us, but we cannot make it. We can only spare it." - David R. Brower

VIVEKANANDA MONASTERY AND RETREAT

6723 122nd Avenue
Ganges, MI 49408
(616)543-4545

A branch of the Vivekananda Vedanta Society of Chicago. Situated on 108 acres of land, the Vivekananda Monastery and Retreat offers a quiet rural setting with facilities for individual and group retreats. In addition to regular classes, the Retreat has a regular schedule of conferences, concerts, and meditation workshops. For more information contact the Retreat Director.

ZEN BUDDHIST TEMPLE

1214Packard
Ann Arbor, MI 48104

(See listing under Canada.)

MINNESOTA

LINDEN TREE COMMUNITY

Rt. 2, Box 133
Underwood, MN 56586

Four-year-old intentional community in west-central Minnesota. Six adults, three children, actively seeking new families, individuals to share in our community. Individual homes, communal ownership of 100+ acres of mixed farmland/forest. Have large central kitchen/activity center. Are establishing truck farm business, Sav-Energy company, educational services, and are open to any 'good work' focuses. We are creating a non-sexist, non-ageist, cooperative environment, and are open to all inquiries and/or ideas.

(See "Articles" section.)

MISSOURI

EAST WIND COMMUNITY

Box CRS6
Tecumseh, MO 65760
(417)679-4682

55 adult members, seven children; plan to grow to 350. Goals: to be egalitarian, non-violent, non-sexist, non-racist, noncompetitive in a gentle culture based on cooperation, equality, and environmental concern. Stress open communication and creative problem solving, and distribute responsibility and authority to empower all.

In 1974 bought 160 acres, also lease 200 more which is government land. This is used for agricultural endeavors as we produce most of our own beef, vegetables, and eggs. We are economically self-sufficient. Industry is rope hammocks and other rope products, and a large peanut butter business for Midwest co-op market. We hold land, labor, businesses and other resources in common, and have a labor credit system for distributing work equally. Open to visits from adults of all ages, limited space for children. We prefer to schedule your visit since our visitor space is limited, so please do write in advance. Please write something about yourself, and when you would like to visit. Our regular visitor period is for one month.

THE GREENWOOD FOREST ASSOCIATION
Star Route, Box 69
Mountain View, MO 65548

Greenwood Forest is a special community of concerned individuals evolving under a common covenant to promote good stewardship, land and forest management and ecology sense for the Ozark Bio-region. Forty families share in common 600 acres in addition to owning their own 5 or 10-acre homestead. Approximately 10 families now inhabit the forest. A community center is being planned at this time. This is remote rural property bordering the Jacks Fork River. Several homestead areas available through private owners/homesteaders. The GF community is handling and channeling any sales through Don Wilson, Star Route Box 70H Mountain View, MO 65548

MONITEAU FARM
The Spiral Inn, Inc.
Route 1
Jamestown, MO 65046

Moniteau Farm is a macrobiotic homesteading community. Twenty-five private land tracts, one 60-acre community parcel, total 400 acres. Seeking harmony through closer relationship to the land, balance in diet and lifestyle, and growing our own food. Diet centers around grains, vegetables, and beans, avoiding red meat, dairy foods, sugar, chemicalized foods. No illicit drugs.

Most members building homes, home industries, and cooperatively home schooling. Established 1980. Landowner's Association approves land use. Some tracts still available. Interested visitors welcome to camp up to five days. Write for more information.

SANDHILL FARM
Route 1, Box 155-H
Rutledge, MO 63563
(816) 883-5543

Est. 1974. Five adults, two children. 135 rolling acres in northeast Missouri; 75 acres cleared, 60 acres mixed hardwood forest. Certified with organic Crop Improvement Association. Grow most of own food. Cows and poultry supply dairy, eggs, and meat. Dogs and cats for pets. Build own structures. Value self-sufficiency and voluntary simplicity.

Total income sharing. Make money from sorghum syrup, honey, tempeh, horseradish, and other food products. Also operate Community Bookshelf, a mail order bookselling business featuring titles on community and cooperative living (write for free catalog).

Though not formal or structured, spirituality is felt in respect, love for earth, each other and other living things. Children especially important in our lives. Time to work, play, be silly and solemn. Enjoy swimming, skating, walks, sweats, crosscountry skiing, art, woodworking, singing and dancing. Looking to grow (perhaps to 12 adults plus children). Like to have visitors, especially during the sorghum harvest in September and October. Write or call ahead to make arrangements. Active participants in the Federation of Egalitarian Communities.

SHEPHERDSFIELD
R.R. 4, Box 399
Fulton, MO 65251
(314) 642-1439

Shepherdsfield is a Christian fellowship which tries to live as the Early Christians did and as recorded in the Acts of the Apostles. This 'Apostolic Christianity' included "sharing all things in common". We have accepted Jesus Christ as the Way, the Truth and the Life. Through Him we have found answers to the many questions that arise in trying to live together and reaching out to others.

At this writing, we have about 100 souls associated with our community. We are located in a farming area outside the city of Fulton, Missouri and within driving distance of Columbia and Jefferson City, Missouri.

We earn our living through an organic bakery, a commercial wall-papering and painting company, several small cottage industries and some printing and publishing. We have a large ministry that reaches over the world in studies of Scripture and principles of Life.

We operate our own school for all our children and take the task of raising children in an environment of 'purity and childlikeness' seriously.

If you would like to visit us, please write or call in advance. We have varying lengths of visitations, before a person may apply to become a novice, which can eventually lead to becoming a member.

WEST WALDEN FARM
R. R. 1, Box 225
Anderson, MO 64831

Individuals/small families enjoying farm work, family fun, growing our own food, caring for each other lovingly, on the premise of 'right livelihood', stimulating reading and discussion, homestead living could find a permanent home here. We need stable mature people of all ages, preferably with building skills, steady income or some capital to invest. No heavy problems, drugs, booze, unhealthy or radical attitudes.

MONTANA

LYLE OLSEN
Box 38
Eureka, MT 59917
(406) 889-3452

Our four-family mountain community has a 15-acre share available, including an unfinished 1200-square-foot two-story house. We believe that cooperation is the key to an enjoyable homesteading life. We share a five-acre lake with 20 acres of marsh, a sawmill, and a dozer and we trade for the use of each other's tools. The 15-acre share and house with phone (no commercial power is available) will cost our next good neighbor about $15,000 (negotiable).

VALLEY VIEW CHRISTIAN FELLOWSHIP
305 Smith Lake Rd.
Kalispell, MT 59901

An outreach oriented community following Jesus' Gospel of Peace. We are peacemakers and oppose violence toward mankind. We believe in the Holy Scriptures and in the Holy Spirit's guidance and empowering; uphold the sacredness of marriage, and practice modesty. Have school for grades 1 - 12. We welcome you. Contact: Roman Miller or Tom Lundgren.

NEVADA

META TANTAY
P. O. Box 707
Carlin, NV 89822
(702) 754-9928

Meta Tantay is a non-profit corporation whose purpose is the revival and preservation of traditional Native American lifestyle and culture. We are located on 262 acres of land just east of Carlin, Nevada. There are people here from many tribal, national and racial backgrounds. We are attempting to build a world for the future generations where we can be at peace with the Mother Earth--without the use of any drugs or alcohol.

NEW HAMPSHIRE

ANOTHER PLACE Mettanokit Community
Route 123
Greenville, NH 03048
(603) 878-9883 or 878-3117

Mettanokit Community is a group of people seeking by mutual support to be an alternative society based on trust, cooperation, freedom and appreciation. We have affirmed our commitment to create the environment of our highest common vision.

We are approximately 12 folks living in southern New Hampshire on 15 acres (about 50 miles from Boston). We manage several cooperative businesses, share income, childcare, housecleaning, work, play. Decisions are made by consensus. We welcome visitors and potential new members. Please call or write first.

GREEN PASTURES ESTATE
Ladd's Lane
Epping, NH 03042
(603) 679-8149 or 679-8282

Est. 1963. The New England regional center for Emissary Foundation International. Weekend, one and three week seminars and classes in the Art of Living. Eighty residents on 240 acres. Organic gardening, wood heat, farming with Belgian horses. Focusing on the requirements for true spiritual leadership in today's rapidly changing world. Well integrated inter-relationship with local government, schools and businesses.

NAMASTE GREENS

RR2 Box 578
Barnstead, NH 03225

Namaste is focused on a living healing dynamic (sharing-caring) in small intimate extended families on land trusts--around green values, e.g., marketplace democracy, integration with nature, social harmony, global justice and sustainability. Seek more family.

NEW MEXICO

LAMA FOUNDATION

P. O. Box 240
San Cristobal, NM 87564
(505) 586-1269
M-F, 9-11 a.m., MST

Est. 1968. Serves as an instrument for awakening individual/collective consciousness. Residents follow different spiritual paths, understanding that all beings and paths are One. Self-supportive through offering summer retreats with visiting teachers, silk-screening prayer flags, and publications. Two hermitages for rent, year round. 110 acres in forested mountains, wood heat, outhouses, limited electricity. Closed to visitors October-April, otherwise open to visitors on specified Sundays. Family/single dwellings, structured daily schedule, communal meals, work, prayers, meditations, song and dance. Open to new members. Write or call for details.

SANTA FE COMMUNITY SCHOOL

P. O. Box 2241
Santa Fe, NM 87501
(505) 471-6928 or 471-3912

Santa Fe Community School is a community which welcomes children. We teach our own and help each other grow. Currently eight adults and nine children, we are expanding and forming an affiliation with new members on larger property in Colorado where we can farm. Solid organization based on consensus decision-making, personal growth through problem-solving with group support, and low cost through cooperation and work exchanges make this community possible for anyone. We welcome visitors (by arrangement) and hope they will want to become members.

WATER CREEK COOPERATIVE VILLAGE

c/o Tuss Callanan
P. O. Box 8938
Santa Fe, NM 87505

Est. 1981. Four seekers/frontiers people want 15+ to join them on their 150 acre farm near the town of Coyote, 70 miles northwest of Santa Fe, New Mexico. Bound together by common commitment to wholistic spiritual practice, stewardship of land, family, growth within community. Largely vegetarians, no drugs, monogamous, uphold nuclear family. Tools, resources, jobs, child-rearing shared, but all have own living/eating space. Equal partners in ownership of land, each share costing $12,000. Surrounded on three sides by National Forest, year-round stream with water rights, fruit trees, large organic garden, grain fields, large community center farm house. Visitors welcome, but need to write at least one month in advance.

NEW YORK

THE ABODE OF THE MESSAGE

Box 300
New Lebanon, NY 12125
(518) 794-8090

The Abode of the Message is a community of adults and children living together, united by ideals of friendship, cooperation and respect for all of life. As an inspiration of Pir Vilayat Khan, a Sufi meditation master, the Abode was founded in 1975 with the purchase of a former Shaker community in New Lebanon, New York. It is situated on 450 acres of mountain and pasture lands, a site held sacred by the American Indians who were its first inhabitants.

The Abode was started in order to provide an environment conducive to the fulfillment of human potentialities, a way of providing a supportive and creative framework within which self-discovery would be fostered. It was formed as an experiment, through a hope that individuals of varying beliefs, interests and desires could live together harmoniously and successfully, learning how to cooperatively share the bounty which life offers, discovering and appreciating the joy and miracle of approaching life with an attitude of love and respect. It is this vision, this ideal, which is a continually renewed purpose and goal of the Abode of the Message.

Visitors welcome, please call ahead for reservations. Overnight guest fees are $11 per adult and $5.50 per child over two. Membership involves a one-month trial period; new members pay a $500 admission fee.

The Abode is currently 60 adults and 25 children. The nuclear family is maintained and the parent/child relationship is strongly nourished. Children are important in all our lives.

ADIRONDACK HERBS
P. O. Box 593
Broadalbin, NY 12025
(518) 882-9990

Small non-sectarian community welcoming folks that follow different spiritual paths or none at all. A basic requirement is a commitment to conservation in the field of the environment, energy, and resources. Our income derives from the sale of herbs to health food stores. Depending upon your abilities, you might have the choice of working with herbs, bees, greenhouses, building construction and repair, hydroponics, electronics, vehicles, alternative energy projects. Choose from different levels of involvement, from guest status (16 hours of work/week) to full-time partnership. If you work more than 16 hours per week you share in the profits of the farm. Diet: vegetarian or not, plenty of fruit, nuts, cheese, tofu, tahini, squid, and weird stuff like that. No heavy drinking, drugs, or hunting. Location: 40 acres in Adirondacks, minutes from Great Sacandaga Lake (great sailing), close to wilderness, skiing, Saratoga Springs, railroad. Cold winters, private rooms or cabins, good library (science, technology, literature, history, 50 journals and magazines).

CAMPHILL VILLAGE U.S.A., INC.
Copake, NY 12516
(518) 329-7924

In Copake, New York, is an intentional community of some 200 people, about half of whom are mentally handicapped adults. It is situated in a rural area 110 miles north of New York City, on 600 acres of wooded hills and farmland. The Village includes farm buildings, workshops, a community center, a giftshop, a co-op store and 17 family-sized houses. Each household is a self-contained residence shared by six to eight mentally handicapped adults and two to four co-workers with their children.

The Village in Copake is part of the wider Camphill Movement which works Educational and Social Therapy with mentally handicapped children and adults. Whether in a residential school for children, a training center, a village with some adults, the fundamental task is the same: to build communities which uphold in each individual the integrity of the Image of Man.

Like all the centers of the Camphill Movement, Camphill Village owes its existence to the innovative therapeutic work of Karl Koenig, M.D. (1902-1966). The philosophy which forms the basis of that work is found in the teachers of Rudolf Steiner (1861-1925) and is known as Anthroposophy. It might be characterized as a path of understanding Man in his relation to both the physical and the spiritual world, compatible with modern western man's thinking and world concepts.

DAYSPRING COMMUNITY
RD#1, Box 176
Himrod, NY 14842
(607) 243-8868

We are a community of about 20 people in one of the Finger Lakes in New York state. We share all things in common, drawing our income from organic agriculture--vegetables and fruits--along with processing & retail sales. We have a school for children grades K-12. The base of our community life is spirituality and a psychological work aimed at helping each other develop and mature. We are working toward setting up a healing center here in the future. Our scope is international. We sponsor a chamber music series. We are involved in the hospitality industry and are expanding our gourmet restaurant endeavors. We are especially interested in networking with other communities in the U.S. and abroad.

THE FELLOWSHIP COMMUNITY
241 Hungry Hollow Road
Spring Valley, NY 10977
(914) 356-8494 or 8499

Rudolf Steiner Fellowship Community--a care community centered on the care of the aged and extending care to the handicapped, youth, and the land. Intergenerational community of 125 people with extensive bio-dynamic gardens, an active medical practice extending into the wider community, a publishing house and print shop, a weavery, candleshop, pottery, woodshop, metal shop, beehives, sheep pens, a chicken house, a greenhouse, a scientific laboratory, darkrooms, sewing rooms, a bakery, and the beginnings of a therapeutic center for baths, massage, and other curative and therapeutic work. Many members are nourished by their study of Steiner's work; others do not have a conscious connection with his spiritual science. The community is non-denominational, but an actively seeking spiritual life provides its foundation. Members make a true effort to work with others in an atmosphere where patience, tolerance and, finally, love are able to unfold in a way that can create deep and abiding bonds.

THE FOUNDATION FOR FEEDBACK LEARNING

139 Corson Ave.
Staten Island, NY 10301
(718) 720-5378

Located in New York City, six of us moved here from San Francisco in 1980. We pooled our resources to buy and remodel a comfortable old 14-room house. By 1984 our number had tripled and we had acquired and renovated three more buildings. Our ages range from two to 63. Most of us are between 30 and 45. We have no common religion, spiritual orientation or philosophic dogma. Nevertheless, we consider ourselves intentional because we do share a decision to pool our resources, communicate every time there is a problem, and contribute to each other however we can whenever possible. Many of us work in town.

Because we are situated on top of a hill rather far back from the street, we have a nice view of the Bay, and an unusual amount of privacy for New York City. The land between the houses is large enough for many trees, flowers, vegetable gardens, fireplaces, and outdoor eating space. We have six open porches and enough room to sit around and talk, play, party or just retreat, outdoors as well as in.

We are expanding a bit right now and are interested in finding a few more people who want to join our kibbutz-like living situation, either on a temporary or a permanent basis. Perhaps some kind of exchange arrangement could be worked out between people wanting to visit for a while.

(See "Articles" section.)

MATAGIRI SRI AUROBINDO CENTER

Mt. Tremper, NY 12457

Est. 1968. Small community near Woodstock whose purpose is to provide a field for the practice of Sri Aurobindo's system of integral consciousness. Publish *Collaborations*, a quarterly devoted to evolutionary vision. Visitors are required to follow daily work schedule and give one-third of their time to assigned work. Tasks include cleaning, construction, painting, gardening, office, kitchen work, etc. Diet is vegetarian with dairy products and fish included. There are regular collective meditations and readings. Matagiri is not a retreat.

RIO BONITO COMMUNITY

Box 73
Uniondale, NY 11553

(See listing under Central America.)

SIVANANDA ASHRAM

Yoga Ranch Colony
P.O. Box 195
Woodbourne, NY 12788
(914) 434-9242

Founder: Swami Vishnu Devananda, Sivananda Yoga Vedanta Centers.

Daily meditation, yoga asana, chanting, vegetarian meals. Come as a guest, resident or karma yoga volunteer (this last requires a six-month commitment). Annual Yoga Teachers Training course. Focus on five basic points for radiant health and inner peace: proper exercise, proper relaxation, proper breathing, proper diet and positive thinking and meditation. Has sauna, pond and cross-country skiing. Located in the Catskills Mountains. Brochure available. Ashrams also in Canada, California, the Bahamas and India. Centers in many major cities.

TURTLE CREEK FARM

651 Halsey Valley Rd.
Spencer, NY 14883

We are a not very intentional group of four people that own a 105-acre farm located 20 miles south of Ithaca, New York. We aren't actively looking for new members, but do have room for one or two apprentices to share work in trade for room and board. We grow plants and vegetables for the local Farmer's Market and keep an assortment of livestock, and do some general farming: all part-time, organically, small-scale, alternatively and chaotically. SASE requested from correspondents, please.

YOGA SOCIETY OF ROCHESTER

93 Spruce Ave.
Rochester, NY 14611
(716) 235-1810

While we are not exactly an intentional community, we are community oriented and have a strong emphasis on education, personal growth and cooperative alternatives.

Actually, The Yoga Society has two identities: firstly, we are a membership organization consisting of people who are interested in their own personal development mainly through yogic practices, as well as through other modalities. We have 200+ paid up members and an active mailing list of 1,250. Secondly we are a core group of six adults and one child who live together in the Yoga Society Center. We have a minimum of formal organizational structure and operate by consensus of the core group.

Our facilities consist of a large house in an urban setting close to the university. We have an extra lot, adjacent, which we use as garden and yard space.

We are always interested in expanding our membership and sometimes have openings in our core group. We can accommodate a small number of visitors for brief periods of time and can arrange special programs (which can be residential in nature) for groups up to 20.

NORTH CAROLINA

CELO COMMUNITY
1901Hannah
Burnsville, NC 28714

Celo Community is a self-governing land trust community, non-sectarian, non-partisan, located in the Black Mountains of North Carolina. Founded 1939, comprises 1,200 acres, includes about 30 member families who make their livings independently; craftspeople, teachers, doctors, etc. Accepts occasional new members, but does not seek them. Activities in the community include: Camp Celo for ages 7-12, the Arthur Morgan School (boarding and day) for grades 7-9, Celo Press, Celo Health Center, Celo Inn, a food cooperative, a retail crafts outlet, and "Cabin Fever University" through which members exchange knowledge and skills. These activities are fully shared by the surrounding community.

THE HEALING ORDER OF THE SUFI ORDER
Rt. 2, Box 166
Leicester, NC 28748
(704) 683-4691

Write for information on Light of the Mountains Community and also for information on other Sufi communities.

LONG BRANCH
Environmental Education Center
Big Sandy Mush Creek
Rt. 2, Box 132
Leicester, NC 28748
(704) 683-3662

Small group of people living cooperatively and stewarding 160 acres of mountainous land, including six acres of gardens and buildings (three passive solar homes, three composting toilets, two passive solar attached greenhouses and a passive solar classroom building, sweat lodge, barn, trout pond, French Intensive garden, berry patches and a large orchard.) Concerns are problems of population growth, natural resources depletion, environmental degradation. Focus is demonstrating specific, practical strategies by which individuals can simplify their lifestyle and become more self-reliant with organic gardening, ecological agriculture, solar energy and appropriate technology. Goals: to be a good example in caring for each other and the earth, research experiments in building and agriculture, and teaching what we have learned to heal the earth. Host visitor programs, weekend workshops, internships and are involved in outreach. Located 25 miles northwest of Asheville, North Carolina, in the Newfound Mountains.

SHALOM COMMUNITY
6017 Bush Rd.
Brown Summit, NC 27214

Est. 1974. Community/housing cooperative on 46 acres of woods and lake, close to Greensboro. More involved in urban careers and service organizations than in living off the land, but dabble in gardening, solar energy, building projects. Interests: education and social work, wilderness adventure, political activism, computers and music. Small, but interested in gradual expansion. Only a few teenagers at home who attend the county schools. Now have one baby. Children mainly raised by parents, with help from community members. Visitors need to write first, in detail about themselves and why they are interested in us (no form letters, please). Our space for new members is limited, but we will try to find housing close by.

OHIO

A.S.
P. O. Box 655
Mt. Vernon, OH 43050

A Mother Earth type survival community in central Ohio with shooting range, great hunting area, farm plots and self-sufficient working way of life would like to correspond with others, exchange ideas, and enlarge our organization. We are accepting residents, $2,000 per acre, and non-resident memberships. Write telling something about yourself, your goals and what you have to offer. Include phone number.

HELPLESS FAR COMMUNITY
Rt. 1, Box 199D
Amesville, OH 45711
(614) 448-4894

Nineteen people--men, women, children. Goals include social change, regional and local self-sufficiency with appropriate technology. 230 acres, several good buildings and an open community spirit. Work actively against sexism, racism, ageism. Two hours southeast of Columbus, Ohio. Come and feel welcome.

LAUGHING BUDDHA FARM
Rt. 1, Box 95
Amesville, OH 45711
Attn: Yeshua

Laughing Buddha Farm is a newly-forming community in Athens County, Ohio (Appalachia). Primary focus for the community is to provide an environment for people with a strong spiritual commitment to nurture their inner and outer unfoldment. Lifestyle is rural/urban. Our area is rich in intentional communities and has a strong support network for alternative lifestyles, as well as a well-established social change network.

OUR KIBBUTZ
c/o L. A. Murray
R.R. 1, Box 728
Ewington, OH 45686
(614) 388-8474

We are a small back-to-the land group. We are located in southern Ohio. We believe in polygamy, but we have no formal organized religion at this time. We are still growing. We are a hard-working, survival oriented group. We are looking for ladies, couples, families, of all races, creeds and religions. Hard working non-pushy people are welcome to contact us. We will be happy to answer your questions.

SUNFLOWER FARM
c/o Bruce Sabel
Rt. 1, Box 90
Amesville, OH 45711
(614) 448-6688

Est. 1975. Seven families on 100 acres in Southeast Ohio, near Ohio University, enrollment 15,000. Each family has a private five-acre homesite, plus there is a 50-acre commons and buildings for community activities, including income projects. Members often have outside jobs. There are a wide variety of skills including artisans, engineers, computer specialists, social service workers and teachers. Plans for an Intermediate Technology School where people can learn food, shelter and alternative energy production skills for more self-reliant and cooperative living.

Adult ages are 30's and 40's, 11 children, the oldest is 15. Some activities we do together are gardening, orchards, laundry, dining, community meetings, childcare programs, stained glass, & woodworking. Seek folks who value a lifestyle of creative independence and interdependence. We ask interested people to please write us about yourself and your interests.

THE VALE
c/o Jane Morgan
P. O. Box 207
Yellow Springs, OH 45387
(513) 767-1416

The Vale is a group of 10 families living on 40 acres of mostly wooded land near the small town of Yellow Springs, home of Antioch College. The Vale is family-oriented. Members, living in their own homes, earn their own livings in town, raise children and gardens, and manage the land and utilities together.

The two members who ran the Vale elementary school for 32 years have discontinued it. The school building is available for either a school or for a small family to occupy.

We govern by consensus. Many of us are Quakers, some of us are vegetarians. Interested in people whose concerns are nature, society, and the family unit. One year's residence is required before a mutual decision about membership is made.

OREGON

ALPHA FARM
Deadwood, OR 97430
(503) 964-5102

Alpha Farm is a close-knit, extended-family-style community on 280 acres in the Coast Range of Oregon. Consensus, our decision-making process, is also a metaphor for the ideal world we seek to create here-- and so help create in the larger world. We seek to honor and respect the spirit in all people and in nature: to nurture harmony within ourselves, among people, and with the earth; and to integrate all of life into a balanced whole. We value service, and work as love made visible. Group process is a strong point: we meet regularly for business and sharing.

Founded in 1972, we average 15-20 adults, and now have three young children. New people spend a year as residents (trial members) before committing to membership. Members and residents work on the farm, in community-owned businesses--a cafe/bookstore, contract mail delivery, and construc- tion--and in freelance professional work. We also offer workshops on consensus and facilitation several times a year. All income and resources are held in common. Individuals have private rooms: other living space is common, and evening meals are communal.

We are open to new residents: visitors are welcome for a three-day initial visit. Please call or write well ahead.

BREITENBUSH HOT SPRINGS
Retreat and Conference Center
P. O. Box 578
Detroit, OR 97342
(503) 854-3314 or
Message (Salem Office) (503) 371-3754

At this time our community is at its full capacity. Even though this is true now, we are always open to hearing from interested beings.

Our work exchange program gives people a chance to experience community life at Breitenbush. Please contact us for more information.

(See "Articles" section.)

CENTER FOR WELL-BEING
82644 Howe Lane
Creswell, OR 97426
(503) 895-2953

We are a small, spiritually-oriented rural community near Eugene, OR. We are committed to personal growth, spiritual development, emotional sharing, connecting with the land and organic gardening. We're slowly developing into a seminar focusing on wholistic healing. Most of our residents have a strong interest or background in healing and country living. We have a Jewish flavor, but practice and appreciate many spiritual approaches. Physical description: 13 acres, goats and chickens, two large houses, cabins, woodshop, greenhouse, orchard, pond and meeting hall. Please write or call before visiting.

CERRO GORDO COMMUNITY
35401 Row River Rd.
P. O. Box 569
Cottage Grove, OR 97424

Cerro Gordo is a community of residents, future residents and supporters who are planning, financing and building an environmentally sound, human-scaled new town for 2,500 people on 1,200 acres near Eugene, Oregon. Homes, businesses and community facilities will be clustered in and near a pedestrian village, preserving 1,000 acres of forest and meadow in its natural state. Private automobiles will be replaced within the townsite by community transit, bicycling, walking, horseback and a community delivery service. The community will recycle materials and rely upon sun, wind, water and biofuels for power as much as possible. The community plans to be self-supporting, with jobs provided by light production companies, education and publishing, community shops and intensive agriculture. The town school will involve community people in providing learning opportunities for the children. While homes and homesites will be privately owned, all residents will be members of the Cerro Gordo Cooperative, Inc., which will own and maintain community open space and utilities and facilitate community decisions and activities. The community building process emphasizes participation in a diverse, yet mutually supportive, community. Cerro Gordoans are seeking to build a neighborly community living in harmony with the natural environment.

We invite you to take part in our project and our extended community. Send $2 for *Cerro Gordo: Plans, Progress and Processes*, which provides a basic introduction and overview, together with our Visitors Guide.

EARTH'S RISING CO-OP FARM
25358 Cherry Creek Rd.
Monroe, OR 97456
(503) 847-5434

Earth's Rising is a 60-acre cooperative organic farm. Co-operative in the loose sense of the word; we are a group of five adults and four kids who comprise five households, each with separate finances. None of us is generating a self-sufficient income from the farm, though some funds are netted in bedding plants, produce, fruit, goats and mohair products. We cooperate to grow and preserve food, collect firewood and to improve and maintain the farm. We eat together frequently. We have collectively-held ideals of environmentalism, cooperation, peace and com-

munity. We are an Oregon Tilth certified organic farm and believe in an organic, natural way of life.

Life is relatively primitive and rugged. We tell folks who want to visit to come prepared for a quasi-camping trip. We all work hard and can appreciate a helping hand. If you want to visit, please give us a few weeks notice and be prepared to be flexible. Normally, we have a three day limit for visitors and ask ten dollars for the stay per adult. This cost includes sauna, shower and floor space.

JESUIT VOLUNTEER CORPS
(Northwest)
P. O. Box 3928
Portland, OR 97212

The purpose of JVC is to promote justice and peace through direct service with the poor and through structural change. Volunteers commit themselves for one year at a time to do full-time ministry. They strive to build community by a simple lifestyle and mutual encouragement of their service. 21 or older. Male/Female. Without dependents. One year commitment. August to August. Receive room and board, health insurance, stipend. Inter-denominational, but strongly affiliated with the Catholic Church. Needed: flexibility, enthusiasm, sense of humor, commitment to values of community, simple living, spirituality and social justice. (See "Articles" section.)

JVC: East - 18th and Thompson Streets
Philadelphia, PA 19121

JVC: Midwest - P. O. Box 32692
Detroit, MI 48232

JVC: South - 1505 Kane Street
Houston, TX 77007

JVC: Southwest - 1427 12th Street
Oakland, CA 94607

LIBERTY CLUSTER
P. O. Box 5247
Eugene, OR 97405
(503) 345-5626

We are a small group with shared interests in personal freedom (both social and economic), earth stewardship, and polyfidelity (a successful form of group marriage). Right now our base is an urban cluster (in the city of Eugene, population approximately 100,000), and we continue to work to develop a rural base within an easy commute. We are pretty individualistic and we enjoy a consciously-chosen level of voluntary cooperation and communalism. A major project of ours is running an educational non-profit PEP, which provides educational materials and networking for those interested in polyfidelity. Please write for a free copy of our newsletter. We enjoy meeting folks who share our interests, especially if they contact us before arriving in town (although spontaneous contacts can sometimes work out).

LORIEN FAMILY LAND
4940 Butte Falls Hwy.
Eagle Point, OR 97524

We live simply and primitively on this enchanted land space, seeking to maintain a balance between our needs and the needs of the land. Working hard and sharing are intrinsic to our lifestyle. Trying to maintain an anarchistic, consensus form of "government", learning that inner clarity rather than egoism lends itself to group decision-making. Presently we are dealing with the economic reality of paying property taxes, while also attempting to acquire a sufficient and constant supply of water for our family and gardens. Open to new members who share our common vision. Please write before visiting and for more information.

MOUNTAIN GROVE CENTER
Box 818
Glendale, OR 97442
(503) 832-2871

We are a struggling group of six adults and three children. Our homes are situated on 400 acres of land; of which 280 are forested and the remainder lies in meadows with creeks meandering through the valley.

The opportunities are endless here for small cottage industries, including the chance to be involved in the groundwork of developing our community.

The people we are looking for need to have a deep commitment, as we all hope to be able to grow together and live upon this land for a long time. It will take hard work, perseverence, ingenuity and, with a little creativity an income is feasible.

We feel that spirituality is a necessity, although none of us follow any religious denomination. Openness, flexibility, honesty, and a sense of humor would be delightful assets, and for us at the present time--a positive attitude is essential.

We have reached a crucial point here at Mountain Grove. Our past debt (taxes, etc.) is accumulating beyond the capabilities of our existing small population. We will need other families to join us to keep our dream alive.

We want to live among neighbors that can share our love, laughter, hopes and dreams.

If you're interested in hearing more from us, please write a letter about yourself and send along with a SASE.

OREGON'S WOMEN'S LAND
P. O. Box 1692
Roseburg, OR 97470

Oregon's Women's Land Trust is a non-profit corporation founded to recognize that land is a sacred heritage and resource belonging to all people, to acquire land for women who otherwise would not have access, to develop harmonious and ecologically-sound land-based community, and to protect the land from speculation and over development.

Membership is open to any woman in agreement with our purposes who asks to be on our mailing list. We request $3 contribution for the newsletter. Decisions are made by consensus at quarterly meetings which are announced in the newsletter.

We have acquired a 147-acre farm in Oregon (Owl Farm, P. O. Box 133, Days Creek, OR) collectively, thus eliminating owner/tenant power divisions. Women and children can visit and/or live. Women need to have time, space and resources to develop their own culture. We are feminists working against racism, ageism, classism, and we share our love for Mother Earth.

Payments for this land come from contributions, often in the form of monthly pledges, from women across the country. Policy on the farm is decided by the women who live there. Limited housing and some camping space available. Visits and inquiries are welcome. Send a SASE with all correspondence, please.

STILL MEADOW FARM
16561 S.E. Marna Rd.
Clackamas, OR 97015

This recently developing Stewardship Farm is located in the foothills of Mt. Hood, on a bluff over the Clackamas River valley. Fifteen of the 48 acres comprise a plateau surrounded by towering Douglas fir trees, including several 800-year-old giants; the rest of the land is mixed forest and dramatic downhill slopes. The tillable land is primarily on the plateau, although two pastures were recently cleared on the slopes. All farming is organic, using green manures, ground limestone, colloidal phosphate and trace minerals.

Still Meadow is currently growing and drying herbs for the commercial market; these quality products are much sought after. Another interest is the reestablishment of a dominant fir forest.

UNIVERSITY CENTER
90 Thornton Lane #1
Cottage Grove, OR 97424

University Center is a small group marriage, began in '73, reformed in Eugene '84; we do conscious parenting, natural self-healing, primal Yoga, Rebirthing, encounter, dance, herbs, lovenergy, Kids Lib Now books by Oneness Press, focus on home-birth, Goddess-energy, crazyness and circles of agreement, cooperation and spiraling, inspired by heartsongs, meditations, Tantra, Rajneesh, cosmic music and Fullers geodesic geometry. The new Oregon Homeducation Network info Service. We do Skits-o-frenics FiestalTheater of the Absurd psychodrama.

PENNSYLVANIA

AQUARIAN RESEARCH FOUNDATION
5620 Morton St.
Philadelphia, PA 19144
(215) 849-3237 or 849-1259
Attn: Art Rosenblum

We do research, publishing to change world thinking; make war/hate obsolete as slavery. All ages, there is a three-month minimum commitment (after visit). Expenses provided. Scientific/humanistic/intuitive approaches to New Age harmony. Use aircraft to go where it's happening. No smoking or drugs. Learn offset printing, networking. Located eight miles from center city in poor row housing with trees, near large parks, safe area.

BRYN GWELED HOMESTEADS, INC.
1150 Woods Rd.
Southampton, PA 18966
Attn: John Ewbank
(215) 357-3977

Est. 1929. BGH owns 240 acres one mile north of northernmost tip of Philadelphia. Each of 75 families is leasee of two acres, and 90 acres of commonland. Cooperation through voluntary participation in committees, which include teenage children, tenants, roomers, etc. Applicants for membership visit families during several months. If applicant wins 80% vote in secret ballot, approved applicant can then negotiate to buy any house for sale, ($50,000 -$150,000). By living among non-conformists, the freedom to spend salary as desired is enhanced. BGH has hosted Fellowship of Intentional Communities.

THE CAMPHILL SPECIAL SCHOOLS, INC.
A Children's Village
R. D. 1, Box 240
Glenmoore, PA 19343
(215) 469-9236

The Camphill Special Schools is an intentional community for the nuturing of mentally retarded children. Through a 10-month integrated program of schooling, home life, and therapeutic activities, the handicapped children are allowed to realize their potentials in an enriching and supportive environment. Located on 67 acres of open space and woodland. It began in 1963 and consists of 10 extended family homes, a school house, a craft center, a community hall, a therapuetic/medical building and several smaller buildings. Adult population is 55, half permanent members, half newcomers enrolled in the Seminar in Curative Education. Visitors welcome. Newcomers welcome. Both should apply to Mrs. Ursel Pietzner in writing. Applications for Seminar should be made in early Spring for start-up in August.

CAMPHILL VILLAGE
Kimberton Hills, Inc.
P. O. Box 155
Kimberton, PA 19442

Est. 1972. 350-acre bio-dynamic farm, 110 people, some are mentally retarded. Eleven houses shelter "extended families" who work the farm, gardens, orchard, bakery, cheese house, sell surpluses, in small farm store and coffee shop. Always have 4 to 6 agricultural trainees. Strong cultural life (especially music) centers on Rose Hill and involves visitors/neighbors. There are five communities in the Camphill system. Each location is unique, yet all are expressions of overall purpose and ideals of Camphill Community. In addition to creating special therapies and training, Camphill seeks to establish social forms of human interdependence between disabled and non-disabled people in a non-denominational, Christian way of life, allowing each person to evolve to his potential as a respected individual. Thus, the recognition and preservation of the involate spirit and dignity of every person is central to Camphill. Appreciate financial contributions from anyone who can, but don't insist on it.

GITA-NAGARI COMMUNITY ISKCON FARM

R. D. 1, Box 839
Port Royal, PA 17082
(717)527-4101

"Plain living and high thinking" is the motto of Gita-nagari, the Hare Krishna movement's 600-acre farm community in central Pennsylvania's Juniata Valley. Begun in 1975 by the movement's founder, Srila Prabhupada, the community raises crops, protects cows, works oxen, schools children, publishes a farm journal, and lives life in the loving spirit of Lord Krishna's Bhagavad-gita, Gandhi's favorite book of truth. Krishna's devotees love to share, and Gita-nagari has a lot to offer: farm-fresh vegetarian foods, spiritual ecology, bhakti-yoga culture, and deep friendship on the path to self-realization. Weary of the modern wasteland? Visit Gita-nagari and drink deep at the reservoir of pleasure--Krishna consciousness. Hare Krishna!

GREENING LIFE, INC.

R. D. 1, Box 265
Shermans Dale, PA 17090

In 1972, Greening Life, Inc. purchased a 135- acre farm in South Central Pennsylvania for the purpose of establishing a planned community. Working together, we put in roads, a community water system and built our homes.

We follow organic farming practices on the 50 acres of tillable land and in our two-acre garden. The garden produces the majority of our vegetables and our orchard is beginning to provide us with fruit.

The effort to create a balance of cooperative living, with time for individual and family has been a rewarding struggle. Growth in spirit, both individual and community is an important part of our life together. We respect all persons and value their opinions as a voice to guide us. We are interested in sharing our resources and spirit with other individuals and groups.

Come and join us, for a visit or a lifetime! Right now we are looking for somebody who can farm our 50 acres of farmland. It probably won't be a full income possibility in the beginning, but could be developed into a more prosperous future, as a part-time job. So far a non-member neighbor farmer has farmed it, but we really would like to see it being farmed by a member or at least by somebody connected with Greening Life.

THE HIGHLAND CENTER AT RABBITY HILL FARM

R. D. 2, Box 141
Dalton, PA 18414

Rabbity Hill Farm is a small, rural, cultural center that invites your participation in the Highland Center Cultural Project, bringing exciting, creative, educational programs to the Scranton, Pennsylvania area.

For the past 11 years, this small non-profit organization has worked on promoting living in harmony with our environment, our community, our diversified cultural heritages and our natural resources.

Specifically toward this goal the Center has sponsored a variety of activities. There have been children's creative workshops, summer seasons of diverse concerts--dance, theater, poetry readings, and festivals. Several workshops have been held covering such topics as: living with passive solar resources, underground houses and communities.

Rabbity Hill Farm is currently looking for people who would like to make the Farm their home, being members of an intentional community land trust. Especially need one or two people knowledgeable about bio-dynamic farming and gardening to design and manage an overall coherent plan for garden, orchard, woods, pond, fields and needs.

Anyone wanting to specialize in the cultural/workshop aspect of the Center is also welcome.

JULIAN WOODS COMMUNITY

R.D. 1, Box 420
Julian, PA 16844

Est. 1975. 140 acres in the wooded hills of central Pennsylvania, one-half hour from Penn State University. We strive for individual freedom and diversity within a cooperative context. We live in "clusters" (small family-like units). Presently we are 12 adults and four children. We plan to form a legal condominium in which we all share the land equally, but each individual has the deed to his/her living or working structure. Except for our basic responsibilities to the group and to the land, we share our lives as little or as much as we like. We are both rooted and stable, and experimental and flexible. We seek people with skills, knowledge, and a sense of commitment.

KEHILLAT MISHPAKHOT
c/o Ernest & Elaine Cohen
525 Midvale Avenue
Upper Darby, PA 19082
(215) 352-2689

Established 1982. About 15 adults plus children. The goal of Kehillat Mishpakhot, or "Community of Families" is to develop a life pattern which markedly improves upon two aspects of modern American society:

1. Relations of people with each other (Community), and

2. Relation between humans and Planet Earth (Ecology).

Kehillat Mishpakhot was started in Upper Darby (Suburban Philadelphia) because our philosophy is "build where you are". The religious component of this sub-culture is derived from Judaism; basically rational but with the "mystic" dedication to protect and perfect Planet Earth as "stewards of the Creator". Kehillat Mishpakhot is egalitarian and communitarian, but focused on life in (expanded) families.

In some ways, Kehillat Mishpakhot is like a Havurah. We celebrate life-cycle and annual holiday cycle events together. There is an affiliate pre-school, which we plan to expand into a "Family School". In addition, Kehillat Mishpakhot is working to build an appropriate economic project for its members.

We are open to sincere members. Those who wish to know more about our program and philosophy, please write or phone.

NORTHEON FOREST
R. D. 4, Box 517
Easton, PA 18042
(215) 258-9559

Northeon Forest as a focus of high endeavor was founded for--and is nurtured by--those who have chosen to search for inner transformation (through the initiative of Gurdjieff) within the normal context of their daily lives. No aspect of external life is overlooked as a fruitful outer framework for parallel inner effort.

Northeon Forest, in its outward appearance, is a tree farm and wildlife refuge. The forest terrain and turbulent streams offer an environment especially fertile for the practice of inner tasks.

There is a profound obligation to respond to the needs of those rare individuals who are genuinely drawn to the goals of The Search at Northeon Forest. Those who find themselves in this category may intiate the entrance process by submitting a condensed statement providing personal data and an account of their reasons for wishing to undertake The Search at Northeon Forest.

TANGUY HOMESTEADS, INC.
20 Tanguy Rd.
Glen Mills, PA 19342

Founded in 1945, consists of 37 homes on two-acre lots with community roads, a pond, woods, a ballfield, and a Center Building-- 100 acres in all. It is 25 miles west of Philadelphia. Founded as a low-cost inter-racial community, Tanguy is no longer low cost; area land and house values have more than quadrupled in the past 20 years. Community work days, monthly membership meetings, cultural, recreational and social events continue. Membership currently requires buying a present member's house, rental properties are rarely available.

RHODE ISLAND

COPIFAWNA
R. R. 3, Box 189
Foster, RI 02825

Copifawna is an intentional community espousing back to nature lifestyle without giving up the convenience of modern technology. Our purpose is to preserve our 200 acres of land as a balanced ecosystem, with 150 acres reserved for wildlife, agriculture and forestry. Our support is residents and a naturist campground. Non-denominational, non-profit, regarding the Creation and its designed functions as the best source of Divine Revelations, revealed equally to all peoples without dogma or absolute. We are seeking like-minded adult (no children) couples to be a part of this permanent balanced ecosystem. We are open to new members and welcome inquiries and interested visitors to the Ecosystem Preserve at no cost. Visitors to the campground pay usual fee.

PROVIDENCE ZEN CENTER
528 Pound Road
Cumberland, RI 02864
(401) 658-1464

Established 1972. Residential Zen meditation training center. Founded by Zen Master Seung Sahn, author of *Dropping Ashes on the Buddha, Only Don't Know, Ten Gates,* and *Bone of Space.* The Providence Zen Center is the head temple in the United States for the Kwan Um Zen School; three senior teachers are available for guidance. The center is located on 50 wooded acres in southern New England. Facilities include two large Dharma rooms, private resident rooms, a library, and a vegetarian kitchen. There is a daily practice schedule, plus retreats each month of from one to ninety days. Long retreats are held at the Diamond Hill Zen Monastery on the grounds. Public talks and "Introduction to Zen" workshops are held regularly. The residency program is under the direction of Abbot Barbara Rhodes, one of the best-known women teachers of Zen in the country.

TENNESSEE

AGAPE COMMUNITY
Rt. #1, Box 171
Liberty, TN 37095
(615) 536-5239

Agape Community is a mission outpost of the Russian Orthodox Church Outside of Russia. True-Orthodox Christian settlers are encouraged, as are sincere inquirers into the Faith. The Community is situated on sufficient land in the hollows of central Tennessee, some 60 miles from Nashville, to provide living space for a number of families, but such residency on Community land is available only on the premise of a commonality of Faith. Original residence at the Community in all cases is on the basis of short or long-term leasehold, with maintenance of completely separate households and economic bases. In principle, the further development of a more integrated life in community is possible and desirable where the necessary basis in Faith has been established and confirmed. A bimonthly periodical, *Living Orthodoxy,* is published by the St. John of Kronsadt Press, as part of the mission work of the community, as well as numerous tracts and other smallworks. Visitors are most always welcome, but are requested to make contact well in advance of any planned visit.

DUNMIRE HOLLOW
Rt. 3, Box 265A
Waynesboro, TN 38485
(615) 722-5096 or 722-9201

Dunmire Hollow (est. 1973) is a community of about a dozen people sharing 160 acres in a magic hollow in Tennessee. We have fields, orchards, gardens, woods, springs, creeks, a community center, woodshop, sauna, county-wide food co-op, etc. Each family is economically independent; we make our livings in a variety of ways: construction, auto repair, teaching, woodworking, sewing, nursing, truck-driving, small

engine sales and repair, crafts, and from providing for ourselves more directly through domestic economy and barter.

We are interested in communicating with people interested in rural community living. We enjoy visitors; please write for more information or to arrange a visit; include a SASE.

SHORT MOUNTAIN SANCTUARY, INC.
Rt. 1, Box 84-A-NACG
Liberty, TN 37095

Short Mountain Sanctuary (SMS) is a not-for-profit corporation chartered in Tennessee to hold land, and keep it free from private exploitation. SMS also provides a place for its residents and members to undertake projects in sustainable agriculture, wholistic forestry, low-cost shelter, and alternative energy.

The residents of SMS are Gay men and Lesbian womyn, their families and friends. On the land they work on self-sufficiency and celebrate the earth's cycles.

SMS is a working farm with a herd of goats, organic garden, chickens, bee hives, fruit trees, and herb beds. The main structures are a pre-Civil War cabin with additions and a large barn.

Organizational income derives from annual membership dues ($60) and registration fees for two nine-day gatherings in May and October. Residents pay a fixed amount each month for food and supplies.

We use consensus for decision making. *RFD Magazine,* a country journal for gay men, has moved to SMS and is now being published here as a cottage industry. Visitors are welcome but need to write in advance. Daily fees for food and land use are $5.00 for non-members and $2.50 for members.

SUNDANCE EXTENDED COMMUNITY
c/o Ellen Martin
Rt. 2, Box 79
Whitleyville, TN 38588
(615) 621-3395

Sundance is a rural homestead 82 miles east of Nashville, 110 miles west of Knoxville, 40 miles from the college town of Cookeville and 14 miles from a small rural town. It was homesteaded in 1978 with the intention of providing an example of alternative living. Electricity is from solar sources, heat is from wood, water is spring fed and food is grown on the land, purchased from a co-op or grown by friends. Sundance members participate in a land trust of seven acres, joint ownership of other land nearby, a home school group and a food co-operative as well as social activities. Sundance offers a place to connect with craftsworkers, organic farmers, home educators, musicians and people seeking new ways (or renewing old ways) to live in harmony with the earth. Sundance welcomes guests for extended periods, but asks that they come prepared to support themselves. Sundance is not seeking members, but can offer connections to others in the area who are.

TEXAS

RAINBOW VALLEY
Rt. 2, Box 28-10
Sanger, TX 76266

New kind of community in Denton County. We are a rural, earth-sheltered community based on the appropriate technology for this type of lifestyle. We live on 220+ acres with half of this acreage set aside for community use. We are cooperative, ecologically responsible, largely self-sufficient. Lots of approximately 1/2 acre now for sale. Decisions are determined by the Rainbow Valley Property Owners Association. Development of roads/utilities and other community needs are determined by the membership, financed and owned by them. All interested parties are invited to enjoy our rolling hills and self-sufficient lifestyle.

SHEPHERD'S BUSH CENTRE
5416 Gaston
Dallas, TX 75214
Attn: Jay Lang

Our purpose is to offer education, spiritual, cultural and emotional support and guidance for those who wish to become more closely united with the Creative Source, from whom all blessings flow. We offer an alternative to existing lifestyle as well as the opportunity to live truly vital lives. We provide the tools that enable each person to make a difference, both in the world within the world outside themselves. Our goal for the immediate future is to publish new materials on Psychosomatic disorders and to provide a spiritually active counseling and training network for healing and health. We invite you to join us, as true learning never ceases. Ours as well as yours is ongoing. We offer classes and workshops.

"No man ever really finds out what he believes in until he begins to instruct his children."
--Ben Holden

WHITEHALL CO-OPERATIVE
2500 Nueces Street
Austin, TX 78705
(512) 472-3329

Founded in 1949, Whitehall Co-op is Texas' oldest housing co-operative. The 13-member household includes a variety of ages and occupations, and everyone contributes equally to costs and labor. Whitehall is a non-sexist, non-racist, non-competitive living environment. Decisions are made by consensus. Our goals include obtaining intimate, meaningful tribal-familial bonds, emotional support, and spontaneous and planned creation and play. We are learning proper use of resources, non-competitiveness and communication skills.

Whitehall will celebrate its 40th anniversary on August 6, 1989. We are looking for past members, especially from the forties and fifties. Call Jim Ellinger for info.

UTAH

THE BUILDERS
P. O. Box 2278
Salt Lake City, UT 84110
(801) 364-7396

We are a spiritual community rooted in daily group and individual meditation, and the desire to achieve Christ or cosmic consciousness. We share all material assets in common to the best of our ability, and work together for the good of all, in farming, gardening, animal husbandry, crafts, natural food stores and a large demolition/excavation company. Our main community is in northeastern Nevada.

(See "Articles" section.)

VERMONT

KARME-CHOLING
Barnet, VT 05821
(802) 633-2384

Karme-Choling is an environment where people practice and study buddhadharma, the teachings of the Buddha. Residents and visitors to Karme-Choling practice meditation, study the buddhist teachings and work together in a contemporary expression of the 2,500-year-old buddhist tradition. These activities--meditation, study and work--are known as the three wheels of dharma, the central principles of buddhism and of life at Karme-Choling.

Please write the center for a calendar of programs, rates and further information.

VIRGINIA

THE COMMUNITY
2704 N. Pershing Dr.
Arlington, VA 22201
(703) 528-3200 or 528-3204

The Community is a trust-based, intimate family of about a dozen people, as well as a cooperative neighborhood/work community of 50 or so people. We are involved in woodworking, health care, education, greenhouse and outdoor gardening, music, art, and many other forms of celebration. A primary economic activity is running a retail computer business, for we hope to understand and help direct the impact the new technology will have on our world. We share strong spiritual values, but do not follow any one path. (See "Articles" section.)

GESUNDHEIT INSTITUTE
2630 Robert Walker Place
Arlington, VA 22207

Established in 1971, Gesundheit was created as a model to address all the problems in health care delivery in the U. S. For its first 12 years, 20 staff lived together and saw 15,000 people from all over the U. S., never charging money, never accepting third-party insurance, never carrying malpractice insurance. We explored extensively being healthy and inter-disciplinary medicine (straight medicine and all other kinds) and being involved in social action. We also integrated agriculture, performing arts, arts and crafts, nature, recreation, etc. in a country-like setting. For the last six years, we've stopped seeing patients, devoting full time to fund raising and building our dream hospital. We have 310 acres in West Virginia. We are building a fabulous 40-bed hospital-free for all people. We have built one building and have one more big one to go. We need help with fundraising and construction. Dream big.

"The village may then serve as a model, lending its structure to larger social forms such as a city neighborhood or suburban community. It can become the basis of a future society which seeks to strengthen rather than destroy the true image of man."
--Camphill Village booklet

INNISFREE VILLAGE
Rt. 2, Box 506
Crozet, VA 22932
(804) 823-5400

Innisfree Village is an alternative lifesharing community with people with mental disabilities, situated on 400 acres of rolling farmland adjacent to the Shenandoah National Forest in the foothills of the Blue Ridge Mountains. We are 17 miles from Charlottesville, home of the University of Virginia. Approximately 18 Volunteers act as houseparents and co-workers in the bakery, weavery, woodshop, and garden in the Village. In addition, five Volunteers live in Innisfree's two townhouses in Charlottesville, working on pottery and the Learning Center activities. In a natural and humanistic environment, the emphasis is on the people-to-people relationships which develop in the course of daily family living and community sharing. Growth comes at a pace natural and therapeutic for the individual. Volunteer duties include helping with cooking, cleaning, and other household management tasks; working in the work stations; attending meetings and participating in the community process.

Requirements: Patience; experience working with persons with mental and/or physical disabilities helpful but not essential; one year commitment, minimum. Benefits: $130/month stipend, room and board, health insurance, medical expenses (except for preexisting conditions), dental expenses up to $250/year, 15 days vacation at $28 per day, and severance pay accrued at $25/month. To apply contact us at the above address and phone number.

NEW LAND
Rt. 1, Box 175
Faber, VA 22938-9749

The New Land is an intentional community of individual homesites in a rural setting, with access roads, a lake, and adjoining acreage held in common. Residents and landholders who choose to join the New Land do so through experience with the Gateway Program or other programs of the Monroe Institute, which also shares the property. Homes are privately owned. Personal freedom and evolving consciousness are shared values. Occupations and lifestyles are a matter of individual choice. Members get together as desired to share in special projects, social affairs, and spiritual growth. Some homesites are available.

SHANNON FARM COMMUNITY
Rt. 2, Box 343
Afton, VA 22920
Attn: Jenny

We found our land in 1974 in a beautiful Virginia valley at the eastern base of the Blue Ridge Mts. Our 58 members (21 women, 23 men, 14 children) range in age from infancy to 65+ years. Most of us have been here five years or more and intend to remain, sharing our lives and dreams.

We own our land in common. Though we have built 17 homes we have no lot boundaries, the care and destiny of our 500 acres rests on all our shoulders. This inescapable fact creates an embracing tension which challenges and binds us.

We are deeply committed to an egalitarian society; we use consensus decision-making (patiently), rotate leadership positions, and keep committee membership open at all times. We encourage each other as we discover our own answers, in our lives and our relationships. Eight of our members own and operate a woodworking and cabinetry shop. Six other members manage a microcomputer systems house, also organized as a worker-owned business. Other members hold regular jobs in nearby towns, particularly Charlottesville, Virginia.

Note: we do not practice community-wide income sharing. You will have to support yourself and find a place to live at first.

(See "Articles" section.)

SPRINGTREE COMMUNITY
Rt. 2, Box 89
Scottsville, VA 24590
(804) 286-3466

Est. 1971. 118 acres, simple life built through sharing, cooperation, farming, gardening, orchard work and living lightly. Two houses, garage, barn. Each adult has private room, common areas for cooking, eating, recreation. Non-smokers, vegetarians, omnivorous. Age of five members, mostly in 40's; child 13. Grow hay for our cows, sheep, keep chickens, bees. Tree crops for people and animals. Grow as much of our own food as possible, sell some surplus. Self-supporting with income from outside work. Those at home garden/fix cars and buildings/develop appropriate technology. Looking for members, especially with children age of ours. Write for more info, visit.

TWIN OAKS COMMUNITY
Rt. 4, Box 169 (CR9)
Louisa, VA 23093
(703) 894-5126

Twin Oaks is a community of 80 poeple living on 400 acres of farm and forestland a hundred miles from Washington, D.C. Since the community began back in 1967, our wayof life has reflected our values of cooperation, nonviolence, and equality.

We are economically self-sufficient. Our hammocks and casual furniture business provides most of our income, with our growing book indexing collective generating much of the rest. Still, less than half of our work goes into these income-producing areas: the balance goes into a variety of tasks that benefit our quality of life, including cooking, communal childcare, gardening, and milking cows. Most people prefer to work a little at a variety of jobs rather than to concentrate solely on one work area. Several of our members are politically active in issues of peace, ecology, anti-racism and feminism. Since 1983 we have hosted an annual women's gathering ("Women - Celebrating Ourselves"), and since 1986 we have hosted a men's gathering, too.

To arrange a visit, write us first several weeks in advance. Potential members visit for three weeks and later go through a six-month provisional period.

WINGED HEART HOMESTEAD
Route HC 67, Box 171
Alum Ridge, VA 24051
(703) 763-3728

Following is a short description of planned activities of the Winged Heart Homestead. The school added to the homestead will be called The Penny Royal Educational Center, and is in the process of being incorporated. We work closely together with other organizations in Floyd County who have related ideals.

The Penny Royal School will give a number of seminars this summer. Brochures on request. The seminars will be moderately priced and barter arrangements will be given in certain cases. The following topics are planned: psychic attunement--learn to give psychic readings, use telepathy, dowsing, house construction using native materials, sweat lodge ceremony, American Indian native traditions (taught by medicine man), spiritual healings according to the Sufis. We are planning to build a Universal, a combination of temple and theatre, for stage plays, music, healing, Universal worship honoring all world religions, etc.

Members will be accepted on their compatibilities to our ideals of Universality, and active interest in spiritual growth. We prefer families with children.

We emphasize: healthy living, respect for ecology, spiritual growth, research in the area of wholistic healing, different methods of organic gardening and farming. The homestead is 283 acres, with camping facilities under construction. Those who wish to camp out here are requested to make reservations in advance.

WASHINGTON

BEAR TRIBE MEDICINE SOCIETY
P. O. Box 9167
Spokane, WA 99209

The Bear Tribe is a modern-day Medicine Society of teachers. We strive in all aspects of our busy and varied lives, to learn our proper relationship with the Earth Mother, the Great Spirit, and all of our relations in the mineral, plant and animal kingdoms. We share with others those lessons of harmony that we have successfully learned, and we learn as well as teach people about the traditional Native American life, ways and prophecies. To sum up our philosophy in a few words: we strive to practice and teach walking in balance on the Earth Mother.

The Bear Tribe is based on the visions of our founder, Sun Bear, a Chippewa Indian who is a sacred teacher and the medicine chief of the Bear Tribe. We are a non-profit organization which serves the needs of our fellow humans through teaching seminars and workshops on the road, through our Medicine Wheel Gatherings and Intensives, through publishing and marketing books and *Many Smokes*, an Earth Awareness magazine, by offering experimental learning at our Center outside of Spokane, Washington, by networking with other communities, and by maintaining our community as a viable, living experiment in alternative lifestyles.

CHINOOK LEARNING CENTER
Box 57 Clinton
Whidbey Island, WA 98236
(206) 321-1884 or
467-0384 (toll free from Seattle)

Chinook Learning Center on Whidbey Island is a non-profit educational and spiritual organization undergirded by a non-residential, covenant community of people committed to the work of personal and social transformation. We offer workshops and courses, and space for individual and group retreats. An ecological-ly-responsible "village" is growing up around Chinook as people buy land cooperatively and individually. The Chinook Waldorf School is open for grades K-five. Chinook welcomes visitors the first weekend of the month for Workday (Saturday) and Openday for potluck, discussion and networking on Sunday. Call or write for brochure and Newsletter.

CLARE'S HERMITAGE
P. O. Box 293
Deming, WA 98244

A small carthusian-style hermitage in the monastic spiritual tradition of Thomas Merton's approach. One to three year commitment asked with flexible times for deep solitude and silent fasting. Celebration of the Holy Mass is the central focus with eastern meditative yogic and oriental practices combined to root out the ego and purify the system. Then only those who have satisfactorily completed a retreat build a small hermitage (12 ft.) and enclosed courtyard (cost $500.) One needs the support of a small individual cottage industry. Monastic training a pre-requisite. Zen, Tibetan or Catholic. Send a long letter to Fr. Michael (Satchakrananda) and an SASE.

PONDEROSA VILLAGE
c/o Larry/Meg Letterman
195 Golden Pine
Goldendale, WA 98620
(509) 773-3902

An established community based on self-reliance, voluntary cooperation and community togetherness, individual ownership of land and homes. Not a commune nor a cult.

Emphasis on personal responsibility and freedom in all respects. Twenty-one families and single people living here now including 38 adults and 13 children. Twenty energy-efficient owner-built homes built or under construction. Visitors interested in joining the community are welcome--phone call ahead of time appreciated. Self-Reliant Life Seminars. Write for info on community and schedule of Seminars.

(See "Articles" section.)

RAJ-YOGA MATH AND RETREAT
P. O. Box 547
Deming, WA 98244

(Note:) This community exists side by side with Clare's Hermitage in Deming. The teacher is the connecting chakra, but they are separate.

A beautifully wooded Ashram-like community dedicated to the Bodhisattva path and vow. Extended retreats available to serious, well-trained teachers wanting to evolve through to the level of GURUship. Completely secluded, intense, direct and honest describes its aura. Founder is Satchakrananda Bodhisattvaguru who teaches, not by example, but by the FIRE of Negation. Send an SASE.

SKYSONG
3716 274TH, S.E.
Issaquah, WA 98027

SkySong is not an intentional community, although those who live here do live in community with each other. We often use the studio for classes, workshops and individual retreats. We are not seeking people, as our facilities are pushed to the limit, but we are always open to visitors and travellers. After two nights, guests pay $15.00 or offer work/service equivalent for each day they are here. We've had some wonderful guests.

SkySong's philosophy is one of harmony with the environment, with an emphasis on permaculture and a sustainable ecology. We work mindfully, meditatively and joyfully and enjoy sharing time with visitors, even briefly. Please write before coming.

TERAMANTO
10218 147th, S.E.
Renton, WA 98056
(206) 255-3563 or 255-9573

(See "Articles" section for more info.)

TOLSTOY FARM
c/o Rt. 3, Box 72
Davenport, WA 99122

Tolstoy Farm (est. 1963) is an eclectic community stewarding 460 acres of canyon land in six different parcels. About the only thing all have in common is avoidance of chemically-dependent farming methods. The largest piece, 160 acres (Mill Canyon Benevolent Society--MCBS), is corporately owned, with land designated for common use and several leased "homesteads." At MCBS 40% are kids and over half of those childlren of school age are home-schooled. Members earn money working in outside jobs, with some having home businesses. Most homes here are solar electric.

Occasional openings for new member(s) occur when a departing family or individual sells their improvements to move. No profit or capital gains allowed.

Some households will take in apprentices who whish to experience our lifestyle.

We try to respect Mother Earth, ourselves, each other and the world. We believe that individual freedoms and community consensus can co-exist and encourage peaceful communication to solve whatever problems may need to be worked out. We are tolerant, liberal, and ethical. Except for weekly potlucks, we find need for comunity meetings rare --one to six times a year. Those wishing "all your info" should tell us about themselves and enclose an SASE.

TWIN BROOKS FARM
644 Lucas Creek Rd.
Chehalis, WA 98532
(206) 262-3169

Open to folks who are interested in alternative country living. 250 acres owned by Don and Dorothy Smith. Land mostly timber and brush, sawmill to cut lumber (alder, fir), horses, sheep for wool and meat, goats for milk, Great Pyrenees guard dogs, large greenhouse. One acre of berries and garden, and 100 apple trees. Appreciate those with knowledge and skills and willingness to work. No dogs and prefer no drugs; open to children.

WEST VIRGINIA

AGAHPAY FELLOWSHIP
Route 3, Box 111
Moorefield, WV 26836

Want to be First Century Christian Community, having rural location/lifestyle, conserving the planet's resources including eating low on the world food scale, having area/neighborhood contacts including witness and outreach to needy people, having members of all ages, etc. Especially wanted: Single people free from family obligations. But families (including children they may have) welcome. Want to have our own school because of dissatisfaction with public school system. Want our own business(es) to assure members of employment. Want to decide democratically by consensus. No unexpected visits please, but correspond first.

CATHOLIC WORKER FARM

Rte. 1, Box 308
W. Hamlin, WV 25571

Christian, rural, communal, kids welcome, visitors welcome, arrange in advance, consensus government, diet individual choice, mostly organic, relationships unstructured. Write for more information.

NEW VRINDABAN INTERFAITH COMMUNITY

c/o Burton Smith
Route 1, Box 318
Moundsville, WV 26041
(304) 843-1600

Est. 1968. Five thousand acres in the foothills of the Appalachians. Three hundred men, women and children practice spiritual life by engaging in devotional service to God. Residents live in a spirit of joyful renunciation, sending forth a call of spiritual love and truth to the world.

We want to give (and receive) friendship, hospitality, knowledge of God and Self. We want to share something wonderful. Something freely given to us and that we freely give to all: ecstatic Love of God (whether you call Him Christ, Allah, Buddha, Krishna, Jehovah, or...)

Facilities (such as rooms, houses, guesthouse) are plentiful (but simple). Visitors always welcome. Brochure and other information availalbe on request.

WISCONSIN

BOUNTY

RT. #3 , BOX 191AA
NEW AUBURN, WI 54757

We are a community in formation. Presently "we" consists of Steve, (37) Kathy (38), and our daughters Emily (8), and Kate (5). We've purchased nine wooded acres on a 22-acre lake and have commenced building our own home, as well as some structures to be shared by the community. (Including a large solar greenhouse, meeting rooms, summer kitchen, sauna and utility building.)

We envision families or individuals maintaining separate households, but sharing many things, (business ventures, tools, garden, home schooling, etc,) most on a voluntary basis. Building options include; adding your home onto the other end of the greenhouse so as to share water, back-up heat, wind

generated electricity, and holding tank; or building elsewhere on the property.

We do not follow any specific philosophical or religious dogma, but strive to be as self sufficient as possible regarding food and energy. Utilizing innovative and ecologically sound methods of production, we hope to demonstrate the feasibility of year-round energy and food self-sufficiency applicable to our northern climate. We are seeking members to be good neighbors and share the stewardship of the land.

CASA MARIA CATHOLIC WORKER COMMUNITY

1131 N. 21st St.,
P. O. Box 05206
Milwaukee, WI 53205

We are a community of 15 people who have two houses of hospitality for the homeless. We take in four or five families and three single women at one time, and we provide food, clothing and furniture for the needy who come to us for help. We meet every Wednesday evening for prayer and business. We are always looking for new people to help us with the houses. We are committed to nonviolence and social change through public protests, prayer and fasting.

CIRCLE

Box 219
Mt. Horeb, WI 53572
(608) 767-2345

We are a loose-knit community/network of people attuned to various paths of Nature Spirituality-- Wicca, Shamanic Healing, Neo-Paganism, Ecofeminism, Pantheism, and related ways. We operate a publishing house, a small recording company, and a counseling service, among other things. We sponsor local, regional, and national gatherings celebrating the turn of the seasons and honoring Mother Nature. We also hold retreats and seminars on dreams, herbology, spiritual healing, metaphysics, and other aspects of inner development. Our headquarters is presently on a farm we are renting west of Madison. We have been raising funds and seeking out land for the past five years to serve as a new and expanded home for our activities. While we do not have room at our present location to house additional people, we are interested in making contact with others interested in Nature Spirituality, both in the Wisconsin area and around the country. Each Summer Solstice we host the National Pagan Spirit Gathering where folks gather in the wilderness and create a cooperative magical village for a week. A sample copy of our quarterly newspaper describing our network, gatherings, and other work is $2. Free brochure on request.

DOREA PEACE COMMUNITY
Rt. 2, Box 161
Turtle Lake, WI 54889

A group of people who have come together to live Shalom more faithfully. The community unifies as an economic and nurturing group offering hospitality and accompaniment with others in their projects and needs. We believe the most urgent problem facing the world today is militarism and the probability of nuclear war. First priority is disarmament. Our actions include war tax resistance, draft counseling, non-violent conflict resolution, direct action for social change, and education.

We live on 89 acres of mostly-wooded land where we focus on living in harmony with the land. We have passive-solar homes, community workshop, vegetable and herb gardens, orchards, a windmill, meditation huts, and space for sojourners and guests. At the present time we are not open to new members.

HIGH WIND ASSOCIATION
2602 E. Newberry Blvd.
Milwaukee, WI 53211

From an accelerating sense that all of us on the planet are joined in a critical historic moment, a number of people in southeastern Wisconsin came together in the mid-1970's to share common concerns, visions and a feeling of urgency. A procession of seminars and conferences exploring many "knowledge frontiers" was organized by those who later were to found High Wind. Several thousand people were touched.

We dialogued about breaking out of restricting belief patterns and realized for perhaps the first time that through the strength of our individual autonomy we could truly begin to affect the course of human evolution. We also saw that, as the world approaches what many predict will be a period of unprecedented change, there is an imperative to live in harmony with one another and with nature.

However, to honor the earth as a living being whom we can no longer exploit without risk of serious repercussion requires moving from talking to DOING. A small group of us felt literally impelled to try to find a way to live the vision more directly.

We decided to focus on experiments in renewable energy and appropriate technology, at the same time learning to move with greater trust in our own intuition. We wanted to be able to tune into what a new breed of scientists is perceiving--that a consciousness/wisdom interconnects everything in the universe.

In 1980 High Wind received a grant from the U.S. Department of Energy to build a "bioshelter."

(See "Articles" section.)

HOUSE OF LAVENDER COOPERATIVE
4555 W. Juneau Ave.
Milwaukee, WI 53233
(414) 933-3033

"Community House" near the center of downtown Milwaukee. Five-to-seven members, variety of backgrounds, share a commitment to good energy conservation practices, nutritious food, progressive social change, alternative development in our city. Since 1968 have had 40 members--educators, counselors, artists, health workers, students, community activists. Several former members still live in the neighborhood and continue to enrich our lives.

MADISON COMMUNITY CO-OPERATIVE
306 N. Brooks St.
Madison, WI 53715
(608) 251-2667

The Madison Community Cooperative was founded in 1968 to help a number of independent housing and retail co-ops to better serve the community. Today, MCC has 170 members in seven buildings that it owns and is controlled directly by its members.

MCC members strive to support an inter-racial, non-sexist community. Each of MCC's houses is autonomous and unique, MCC being a fairly, decentralized co-op structure. Although situated near the University of Wisconsin--Madison Campus-- MCC encourages people of all ages including single parents and their children to join us. For more information on MCC and other housing co-ops in Madison, call or write us.

MARTHA'S HOUSING CO-OPERATIVE
225 Lake Lawn Place
Madison, WI 53703
(608) 256-8476

One of six houses owned by Madison Community Co-operatives. We're a diverse group of 30 workers and students who strive for a high degree of intimacy and involvement with each other. We are committed to cooperation and consensus, as well as feminism, peace, caring for the environment and many other issues. We share a vegetarian meal every evening, and all interested folks are invited to share our food. We ask a one year commitment of all new members. Children are welcome.

THE TEACHING DRUM

P. O. Box 1892
Eagle River, WI 54521
(715) 479-9292

We exist to provide the environment and the tools to explore and become more attuned to our inner and outer selves. The skills and awarenesses we learn here help us each to know that personal Vision that cries to Dance. We seek instructor apprentices and support staff. Please send 50 cents in stamps for information packet. (See "Articles" section.)

"Most people live in cities. Hence if the condition of the majority be taken as the norm, then normalization must mean urbanization. If, however, normalization be the quest for balance--a confident individual moving securely and usefully among friends in a purposeful social setting--then it were surely foolish to forego the harmonizing, balancing, "therapeutic" effects of the other kingdoms of nature. To create settings in which human beings can live in harmony with a landscape and other living things is an aim higher than mere existence. It can no longer be seen as a utopian escape to a socially irrelevant Garden of Eden; it has become an ecological necessity."--Camphill Village booklet

---

GLOBAL

AUSTRALIA

EMISSARY FOUNDATION INTERNATIONAL
c/o Hillier Park
Hillier Rd.
Gawler 5118, South Australia
(085) 22 2830 or (085) 22 2511

Thirty-five permanent residents. Regional Centre for the Emissary Foundation International in Australia. Spiritual awareness beyond dogma or belief. Directed towards a more effective and creative life experience.

BELGIUM

TUILTERGAERDE
Stokrooieweg 3
3511 Kuringen
Belgium

Commune of seven people in the agricultural area close to the city of Hasselt. Live together on the land and do biological farming. Have an alternative school and support grassroots activities, cooperatives, and collective living initiatives. Have collective management and consensus decision making. Can welcome and host five guests at once.

CANADA

CARAVAN STAGE CO.
R.R. 4
Armstrong, B.C. VOE 1B0
(604) 546 8533

Est. 1970. Living a dream--they travel from town to town by horse-drawn wagon and bring the exciting world of theater to rural residents. Has toured over 8,000 miles through three provinces and played to thousands of people. Each season they hit the road with an innovative and colorful production which can include up to six wagons, 11 Clydesdales, outriding horses, 20 performers and technicians and versatile self-contained performing environment.

Equapolis Farm, 80 acres, is owned/operated by Bill Miner Society. It is where new shows are born, actors rehearse, wagons are built and refurbished. Farm was established in 1978 and placed in trust to ensure agricultural use of the land in perpetuity. All work is done under Clydepower; land cultivated, plowed and sown and in late summer the farm hosts a unique community celebration, the annual threshing bee. Also one of the few breeders of Clydesdale horses in western Canada with two stallions and 10 broodmares. Farm offers clinics in draft horse skills, use of alternative energy and its rural application. Also conducts workshops in theatrical skills such as voice, movement, and scenic art for the novice and advanced.

COMMON GROUND
56 Balmoral St.
Winnipeg, Manitoba R3C 1X4
(204) 775-2750

Est. 1972, 15 members, seven of whom share meals and accommodations in an old 3-story house in downtown Winnipeg. Operates as a lifestyle alternative with no clearly defined philosophy. Enables lower consumption of material goods and improves relationships, among themselves and others. High turnover-rate, but still manages to function and remain a viable alternative. Believe cooperative living is a fruitful experience, for a year or a lifetime. Welcome visitors for short stays and expect only some sharing of food expenses. When there is an opening, new members are accepted by consensus of the present membership.

"And let your best be for your friends. If he must know the ebb of your tide, let him know its flood also. For what is your friend that you should seek him with hours to kill? Seek him always with hours to live. For it is his to fill your need, but not your emptiness. And in the sweetness of your friendship let there be laughter, and sharing of pleasures. For in the dew of little things the heart finds its morning and is refreshed."--The Prophet

---

"Those who desire to create harmony in the world must first establish order in their own communities. For this, they must first regulate their own family life. To cultivate family life they must first cultivate their own personal lives. For this they must first set their own feelings right. Wishing to set their own feelings right, they must first seek to make their own wills sincere. For this, they must first seek to the utmost their own understanding. Such increase in understanding comes from the extension of their knowledge in all things."--Confucius

COMMUNITY ALTERNATIVES CO-OP
Membership Committee
1937 W. 2nd Ave.
Vancouver, B.C. V6J 1J2

DANDELION COMMUNITY
R.R. 1 (CR)
Enterprise, Ontario K0K 1Z0
(613) 358-2304

Est. 1975. Nine adults, two children, sharing goods, income and expenses; self-supporting through own cooperative business (hand-woven rope hammocks and chairs). Aiming at agricultural self-sufficiency on 50-acre farm near Kingston. Raise children communally in a non-sexist, egalitarian environment. Work shared equally through labor credit system, with opportunities to learn new skills. Value closeness as small community; open to new people who share our ideals of non-violence, ecological awareness, feminism, communal alternatives and social change. Write for more information and to arrange visits. (Drop-ins cannot be accepted.)

DRAGONFLY FARM
Lake St. Peter
Ontario, Canada K0L 2K0

Dragonfly Farm is a community of 10 people, living on 248 acres of Canadian Shield in Eastern Ontario. We come from many places; in our background one would find urban alienation, anarchism, scientific rethinking, non-sexism, paganism and generic new age beliefs. The animals, gardens, fields, and woods provide us with dairy products, vegetables, herbs, building materials and heat. Money comes in from a greenhouse operation, crafts, city work and local odd jobs. The land is host to a number of gatherings and we are active in the alternative community around Bancroft. We are learning to live in harmony with and enjoy ourselves, each other and the natural surroundings. Visitors are welcome.

EMISSARY FOUNDATION INTERNATIONAL
c/o David Thatcher
Box 9, 100 Mile House
British Columbia, Canada V0K 2E0

This non-profit organization founded in 1932 is an association of friends which, amidst other activities, operates several large communities and communal homes around the world. These facilities haven't been established to save money, grow organic gardens or pioneer complimentary healing techniques, though there is developed expertise in these areas. Our sense of community is based in love/respect for life and its inherent design. We offer spiritual leadership courses, assist any who wish to reveal their potential, and celebrate the myriad ways in which humankind is awakening to the way life truly works.

FRASER COMMON FARM CO-OP
1356-256th St.
R.R. 4
Aldergrove, B.C.

Community Alternatives is a group of over 50 people--men, women and children--living together in our two residences in Vancouver and Aldergrove (40 miles east of Vancouver), British Columbia. We are working towards an egalitarian, non-sexist, inter-generational lifestyle, sharing resources and using renewable energy systems which enable us to live more conservatively. We recognize celebration and spirituality as an important aspect of community life. At present (June 1985) we have room for two-three adults in the City and another two-three adults on our farm, depending on specific skills they can offer. Landed immigrant status or Canadian citizenship necessary. Write either address above for more information.

HAILOS COMMUNITY
P. O. Box 8
Lumby, B.C. V0E 2G0
Canada

A New Age community of "free-spirited" brothers and sisters from different backgrounds--all seeking truth and happiness along their path--to develop a lifestyle in harmony with nature and based on mutual respect and love--a community where we look for the Oneness beyond our differences.

We're growing most of our own food, and supporting ourselves with our cottage industries on 320 acres in a secluded valley in southern British Columbia.

We're seeking a lifestyle where there is time and room to explore the spiritual and social aspects of life; Hailos is a home for those who share high ideals and who know that tomorrow is built today. For more information or proposal, please write to us.

HEADLANDS
Stella, Ontario
Canada K0H 250

Est. 1971. Non-profit consumer cooperative. Own livestock and garden provide much of our own food. Members involved in a commercial sheep farm and a construction company. As of July 1985 we are four men, two women, three children (ages 13, three and one). Hope that Headlands will continue to evolve towards a larger community of individuals living and working in smaller consumer and producer cooperatives.

KING VIEW FARM
P. O. Box 217
Aurora, Ontario L4G 3H3
Canada

Forty miles north of Toronto, in Kings Township, the "horse capital" of Canada. Terrain is gently rolling and very green. Trees are an integral part of the landscape and provide an essential water balance factor on the farm.

On 97 acres are raised dairy and beef cattle, poultry, hay and grain. During growing season cattle are rotationally grazed to prevent depletion of plants/soil. A three-acre garden provides wholesome food for residents and visitors. A 270-foot hydroponic greenhouse, nestled into a roughland pasture valley, provides two to three thousand heads of fine quality lettuce per week, sold to restaurants/green grocers in the Toronto area by the King View Lettuce Corporation.

KOOTENAY COOPERATIVE
LAND SETTLEMENT SOCIETY
Argenta, B.C. V0G 1B0
Canada

Est. 1971. We are 18 adults and five children living on 200 acres of forested hillside at the north end of Kootenay Lake in southeastern British Columbia. We are striving for a balance of ecology and human economy on our land and in our community. We have a system of 12 individual homesites surrounded by common lands. Prospective visitors must write in advance, there are openings for new resident members, write for details.

MORNINGSTAR FARM
R.R. #1
Berkeley, Ontario N0H 1C0
Canada
(416)851-0139

Small rural community forming, central Ontario. Personal growth in mutual love and respect--sharing and caring with and for each other.

Healthy, active, hardworking couple, early 50's, seek five friendly, caring, tolerant, enthusiastic, committed, like-minded couples to invest skills, labour, capital. Share 232 beautiful acres, scenic rolling land, mature maple and cedar bushes, trout stream, loam soil. Quiet, secluded, but easily accessible.

Buildings include five-bedroom farmhouse, excellent barn, several old outbuildings, four newer utility buildings.

Plans include self-sufficiency, private housing (severances obtained), shared use of common land, cooperative enterprise, cottage industry, etc.

(See "Articles" section.)

STILL MOUNTAIN SOCIETY
R. R. 1
Fernie, B.C. V0B 1M0
Canada

Still Mountain Society is a non-profit educational organization sponsoring programs at White Spruce Farm and workshops throughout Canada. Aim is to become self-reliant and develop a way of life which is ecologically sound and efficient. White Spruce Farm is a "homestead" situated on 250 acres of wooded land near Fernie, B.C. Five acres have been cleared for gardens, homes and the Learning Centre. During summer months, a comprehensive program is presented at the farm. Classes are offered in organic gardening and natural agriculture, natural foods, macrobiotic cooking, herbs and wild plants, folk medicine and natural healing, Tai Chi, Yoga and Shiatsu.

YASODHARA ASHRAM
Box 9
Kootenay Bay, B.C. V0B 1X0
Canada

Est. in 1956 by Swami Sivananda Radha. Moved to Kootenay Bay, B.C. in 1962 on a woodland area of 83 acres, on the shores of Kootenay Lake.

NEW AGE COMMUNITY GUIDEBOOK 103

The purpose of the Ashram is to provide a center of yogic teaching and practice where people may pursue their inner growth in a spiritually supportive environment.

In addition to a teaching program we run a bookstore, recording studio, printshop and publish a journal, *Ascent* twice a year and operate a small farm and orchard.

ZEN BUDDHIST TEMPLE - TORONTO
86 Vaughan Road
Toronto, Ontario
Canada M6C 2M1

ZEN BUDDHIST TEMPLE - MICHIGAN, U.S.A
1214 Packard Rd.
Ann Arbor, MI 48104

Spiritual communities focused on zen training and manual work, under the guidance of Zen Master Samu Sunim of the Korean Chogye Order, living a communal lifestyle on the monastic model as it is adapting itself to North America. Some members hold jobs, others work within the temples on projects including the publication of *Spring Wind--Buddhist Cultural Forum*, our international quarterly journal. The training is open to men, women, couples (under special circumstances, families) and can lead to religious ordination (monk or nun) or lay ordination (Dharma teacher) for qualified individuals. Short visits can be arranged. A 3 month trial residence period and a sincere mind for zen training are prerequisites for full time community membership. Inquiries welcome.

CENTRAL AMERICA

LEONA WELLINGTON
Apartado 7-2030
San Jose, Costa Rica
Central America

Own beautiful 180 acres, partially self-sufficient farm in Costa Rica. Want light industrial community in natural setting. Can sell plots, reasonable, after trial period. Want teachers, families and earthy types. No dope.

RIO BONITO COOPERATIVE
Stan Ross
Rio Bonito Community
San Ignacio P. O.,
Cayo District, Belize, Central America
- or -
RIO BONITO COMMUNITY
Box 73
Uniondale, NY 11553

Our cooperative is located in beautiful, tropical Belize, Central America; an English-speaking member of the British Commonwealth. We are a vegetarian, farming cooperative consisting of four adults and one child.

We strive for self-sufficiency and practice methods of ecologically-sound organic farming in the western mountain region of this tiny, unpolluted country. Our community is free of electricity, T.V. and motorized machinery, thus allowing us to experience a simple, but comfortable lifestyle. We are non-sectarian, nonviolent and there is no use of drugs.

The water and air are pure, the fruits are delicious and the weather is perfect. The government is stable, democratic and welcomes Americans. Our community invites visitors and new members. Children are welcome. Please write our U.S.A. address for more information.

FRANCE

PERMACULTURE PYRENEES
Bouriege 11 300 Limoux
France

Agroecological School. Non-profit making association. Purpose: revival and maintenance of the Autonomous Native European Creativity. Promoting the arts, crafts, ecological agricultures, science. Located in the foothills of the Pyrenees bioregion, with a house in a neighboring village where artistic activities and related workshops are offered to the local, rural population. 100 acres, secluded and difficult access. Building own living facilities, school house and barn under way. Planning windmill, soft-tech pumps, irrigation system. Need funding. Visitors expected to join in work. Open to new members. Write before visiting. Not strictly vegetarians. Hope to grow to a stable group of about 10 adults.

INDIA

AUM SWARUPA COMMUNITY
1170/12 Revenue Colony
Pune 411 005
India

Part of Atma Santulana Village, near Lonavala (130 kilometers from Bombay). Work on different meditation and Yoga techniques, Yoga-based health guidance and ayurvedic medicines and cosmotology sessions and on the personality transforming process. One may share in the life of this village by participating in the Learning or Living community activities which include morning meditation, gardening, individual therapies, course classes and work experience. Eleven members live together to set up the village.

AUROVILLE
Pin 605101
Tamil Nadu, India

Auroville, a developing international township, is currently composed of communities interspersed among 11 Tamil villages on 2,000 acres in Tamil Nadu, South India. About 800 men, women and children, representing 16 countries and servings as volunteers are the core population. Guests, visitors, and new members are welcomed throughout the year. Mother and Sri Aurobindo are the inspiration behind the development of Auroville whose stated aims are to realize an effective human unity and peace on earth.

(See "Articles" section.)

For information about Auroville, Mother and Sri Aurobindo contact: Auroville International - U.S.A., P.O. Box 162489, Sacramento, CA 95816.

INDEPENDENT CHRISTIAN LEAGUE
Mr. A. Kovilpillai B.A., B.T.,
Executive Director
Office at Interfaith Orphanage
Ottapidaram, (pincode-628 401)
Chidambaranar District, India

Rural Christian Community Development Agency running the following Community Development Educational Schools and Orphanages for the welfare of the community: 1) T.M.B. McAvoy Rural Middle School 2) Attached with Interfaith Orphanage 3) and Interfaith Orphanage Rural Junior Technical Training Center where in 1500 orphaned, abandoned, street abandoned, most deserving destitute pupils are fed, clothed, educated in Middle School Course and with simultaneous training in Junior Technical and Mechanical Courses 4) Inter Christian Mission Middle School attached with 5) Inter Christian Mission Orphanage where in 200 children of abandoned nature are fed and educated 6) St. Gabriel Primary School 7) Rural Hospital under construction intended to give free medical for 150 villages but stopped on want of funds 8) Inter Christian Mission Middle School with Nursery Section 9) Gift food aid relief project to increase nutritive aspects of children body of 3500 children of those above mentioned institutions. Interested groups and individuals in the project institutions are requested to contact at the above address.

MEXICO

COMMUNIDAD KRUTSIO
Apartado Postal 174
Guerrero Negro
Baja California Sur
Mexico

Krutsio is an intentional community that explores and opens a more life-giving path of social advancement. The exploration of Krutsio goes beyond basic survival, it is guided by the luminous star of a unified humanity.

Krutsio is located in a small valley between the mountains and the sea. The mountains are part of the Central Desert of Baja California. The sea is the Pacific Ocean. In Krutsio there are not employers or employees. Our community is built and maintained by our own hands. Therefore, in Krutsio we do all sorts of things: agriculture (on a small scale), building, carpentry, cooking, design, education and care of children, food preserving, harvesting, and processing of sea resources, mechanics, solar distillation of sea water, etc.

In order to reconcile the strong work demand with the desire for balanced development, we try to work fewer hours, but make them productive, efficient hours. In Krutsio we work about six hours a day, six days a week. We try to let everyone work in what he/she likes most and does best. The more routine jobs are equally shared or are rotated.

COMMUNIDAD LOS HORCONES

Carretera A La Colorado
Apdo #372
Hermosillo, Sonora, Mexico 83000

Est. 1973. Walden II-type community, culture based on cooperation, compartition, pacifism. Use Experimental Analysis of Human Behavior to achieve these objectives. Thirty people on 45 semi-arid acres. Communal care and schooling of children, also train mentally retarded children. Income is derived from that training, also teach courses, rent tractors, sell crafts. Diet is natural foods, some eat meat. Monogamy is practiced. Many work collectives, recreation and art encouraged. Have several communal buildings and facilities. Want to grow and are open to all persons serious about community life and wanting to build a new society. Write before coming.

NEW ZEALAND

CENTREPOINT COMMUNITY GROWTH TRUST

P. O. Box 35
Albany, Auckland, New Zealand

A spiritual community under the guidance of Bert Potter. Members renounce all personal possessions and make a commitment to Bert, their personal growth and honesty with each other. The lifestyle is close living with up to 10 couples plus small children in one open longhouse. About 160 are currently living in the community, sharing communal dining room, lounge and clothes. A number of businesses operate from the 92-acre, bush-lined property including a tree nursery, pottery, silkscreen printing and other crafts. Psychotherapy workshops are held at the community and at the Counseling Centre in nearby Auckland City. Catalogue available upon request free of charge (donations for postage O.K.)

RIVERSIDE COMMUNITY

R.D. 2 Upper Moutere
Nelson, New Zealand

With over 200 hectare, began as a Methodist farm in 1941. Has evolved to become a Christian pacifist community with over 60 members of all ages. Economically viable with no private property. Focus on wellbeing and limitations of income.

TODD'S VALLEY

Nelson R.D. 1
New Zealand

An area where people with ecological consciousness are creating an alternative. Many people pass through this area, and it is therefore like a center.

SCOTLAND

THE FINDHORN FOUNDATION

The Park
Forres, Scotland EV36 OTZ

Est. 1962 by Peter and Eileen Caddy and Dorothy Maclean. 200 people, all ages who live and work in conscious awareness of the presence of God within all life. Has expanded to include its original trailer site, residential hotel/college, several large houses and custodianship of the Isle of Erraid, off the west coast of Scotland. Also network with other communities. Tapes and literature available. If intending to visit please write, well in advance.

LAURIESTON HALL HOUSING CO-OP

Castle Douglas
Kirkcudbrightshire, Scotland
Phone: Laurieston 275

We are a group of about 20 adults and 10 children living in and around an old mansion house in the heart of Galloway countryside. Founded in 1972. We own about 130 acres of land, live quite independant lives and manage our collective affairs by consensus government at a weekly meeting. We produce a large amount of our own food and dairy products; wood for our woodstoves gathered weekly from local forests. Hydro-electric plant for lighting and hot water. Between March and October we host conferences and events: organising company called The Peoples Centre. About 1500 paying visitors each year. Our own lake, sauna, large conservation area. Two weeks each year for visitors who want to get to know us and experience living here. Other visitors encouraged to come for events weeks, or to help during tri-annual maintenance fortnights. Write for more info.

SWEDEN

COMMUNIDAD

Box 15128
S-104 65
Stockholm, Sweden
Tel: 41 01 47

In suburbs of Stockholm, consists of a group of Latin American exiles who were part of a larger community founded in Uruguay in 1955. Presently 15 members (five children) of different nationalities. Purpose is to satisfy necessities of each member by solitary self-management and anti-authoritarian ways. Principle activities are bi-monthly review in Spanish, printing and editorial work (children's books, political essays, literature...) in Spanish and Swedish.

WEST INDIES

RICHARD PRESSINGER

Lucea, P. O.
Hanover
Jamaica, West Indies

Have recently established a small community/resort facility in the town of Lucea, midway between Montego Bay and Negril. Building is currently underway with strong emphasis on "nonchemical" construction and living. Our plans are to create comfortable living conditions for individuals who are "environmentally sensitive" or who just wish to live in non-polluted surroundings.

Present plans include expanding our organic garden and housing facilities. We are seeking individuals, families, or visitors who strongly believe in the importance of these ideals, as well as the importance of educating others. If you enjoy the ocean, good food and clean air, drop us a line.

Resources

Following is a listing of organizations, networks, institutions, schools and New Age centers which may be of interest to the community-minded. Some are intentional communities who do occasionally accept new members, but usually those members are people who first take some of their courses or workshops, or in some other way become involved with the group prior to becoming new members.

AQUARIAN RESEARCH FOUNDATION
5620 Morton Street
Philadelphia, PA 19144
(215)849-1259

We research ways to a positive future by visualizing the world we want, then finding ways to get there. Publish *Aquarian Alternatives* Newsletter and a book on relationships/natural birth control. Now we're producing "Where's Utopia?", a video on cooperative systems for which we brought a Soviet scientist to visit America's most successful communities. We use a 1958 Cessna for this work. We have two national computer networks to link communities and people changing the world. One is free! With children (ages four and nine) we're now seeking to join a larger community interested in these projects and transforming the nation/world into cooperative systems, a rulership of love. Use no drugs or tobacco; teach printing and flying, open to polyfidelitous group. Aquarian is tax-exempt since 1970, donation supported.

AUSTIN CO-OP RADIO, INC.
P. O. Box 50018
Austin, TX 78763

Texas Educational Broadcasting Co-operative, Incorporated, doing business as Austin Co-op Radio, is a locally-owned, non-profit corporation organized as a co-operative. KOOP-FM seeks to provide high quality, innovative and diverse programming of entertainment, information and education about Austin, Texas, and the world around it. KOOP-FM will provide equitable access for the community to participate in the operation and governance of the station. Austin Co-op Radio is a tax-exempt, educational organization, not affiliated with any religious or political organization.

CHINOOK LEARNING CENTER
Box 57, Clinton,
Whidbey Island, WA 98236
(206) 321-1884 or
467-0384 (toll-free from Seattle)

Chinook Learning Center on Whidbey Island is a non-profit educational and spiritual organization undergirded by a non-residential, covenant community of people committed to the work of personal and social transformation. We offer long and short-term residential and non-residential workshops and courses, and space for individual and group retreats. An ecologically-responsible "village" is growing up around Chinook as

people buy land cooperatively and individually. Chinook's Waldorf School opens with kindergarten in September '85. Chinook is open for potluck, discussion and networking the first Sunday of every month. Call or write for brochure and newsletter.

COMMUNITIES, JOURNAL OF COOPERATION
126 Sun Street
Stelle, IL 60919

Since 1973, *Communities* magazine has reported on the development of intentional communities, from people building together in urban neighborhoods to rural farm communities, with articles on community politics and group dynamics, family life and relationships, health and well-being, work and food cooperatives, and other areas of innovation and expertise developed or applicable to community living. "Reach" and "Resources" columns provide information on individuals, groups, publications, and other community-related organizations and resources. Communities publishes a Bi-annual Directory and Guide issue.

COMMUNITY SERVICE, INC.
P. O. Box 243
Yellow Springs, OH 45387

Publishes a list of Intentional Communities, a newsletter, and also provides many other community-related services, including land trust counseling. It hosts conferences and publishes and sells books.

(See "Books, etc." section.)

EARTHBANK ASSOCIATION
P. O. Box 87
Clinton, WA 98236

Working with alternative economics and social investments. Write for more info.

FARALLONES INSTITUTE RURAL CENTER
15290 Coleman Valley Rd.
Occidental, CA 95465
(707) 874-3060

Farallones was founded in 1974 as a non-profit institute for participatory education and appropriate technology which is efficient, low-cost, locally controlled, and adapted to local needs. Farallones' goal is to integrate that concept into the mainstream of our communities and our lives.

Our two sites--the Integral Urban House in Berkeley, and the Rural Center in Occidental, CA--have pioneered in research and training programs for resource conservation and management, renewable energy sources, and small-scale food production. Our staff and trainees work with a wide range of service agencies and grassroots organizations throughout the U.S., Latin America, Africa, and Asia.

Our programs focus on a variety of skills including: solar energy (design, construction, etc.), wind energy, pedal/treadle power, conservation and weatherization, blacksmithing, alternative toilets, water conservation/collection, organic food production, preservation and storage, woodlot management, and compost. We offer intensive courses, workshops, and seminars, to name a few of our services.

We are located on 80 acres with many demonstration facilities and long-term accommodations. Public tours offered on Saturdays. Not a community open to new members.

Participants in our Educational Programs may live "on site" with staff during the courses. People seeking apprentice positions in Horticulture may apply for six-month terms. Write for more information.

FEDERATION OF EGALITARIAN COMMUNITIES
Box 6B2-H
Tecumseh, MO 65760
(417) 679-4682

A group of intentional communities spread across North America, we range in size and emphasis from small homestead-oriented groups to village-like communities similar to the Israeli Kibbutzim. All of our groups have been in existence 10+ years, one since 1967. A central belief in cooperation, equality, and non-violence brings us together.

Federal communities offer a clear alternative to traditional lifestyles: men and women share nurturing children, making decisions, constructing buildings, preparing meals, and operating businesses.

We value cooperation above competition, and the creation of a healthy, supportive environment above materialistic gains. How we do things is as important as what we do.

If this sounds attractive to you and you'd like more information, write and ask for a brochure ($2 donation requested). All of our communities are seeking growth and generally welcome the opportunity to share their lives with others.

FRIENDSHIP TRAIL
P. O. Box 47068
Phoenix, AZ 85068

Friendship Trail is committed to respond to Your inquiries. F.T. is a provocative, controversial, boot strap adventure in Self-Government. The Use of Force and/or Coercion is Prohibited! F.T. extends northward from Henderson, Nevada to Blaine, Washington State. F.T. is truly a Participatory venture...Your Sovereignty is recognized! F.T. is NOT a religious experiment, nor a political movement. The Causes and Effects on Household Family Units (including children) by Economics is of special concern and is addressed to Individuals with Collective representorial solutions. The Legacy is foretold!

GUIDEPOSTS FOR A SUSTAINABLE FUTURE
P. O. Box 374
Merrickville, Ontario, Canada
K0G 1N0

Guideposts for a Sustainable Future is a project designed to inform and involve the public. The "Guideposts" project is producing an educational kit for distribution through networks of citizens organizations. The kit will consist of a video and a discussion guide. The video presents the challenge of sustainability: an explanation of how this problem has come about, and a set of guidelines indicating the limitations and opportunities of sustainability. The discussion guide will give suggestions about how to set up a meeting around the kit; further details about the material in the video; explanations of major environmental issues; list of things people can do to make their lives more sustainable; and addresses of organizations and networks where information is available and willingness to help would be appreciated.

Activities are sustainable when they: use materials in continuing cycles; use continuously reliable sources of energy and; come mainly from the potentials of being human, i.e., communication, creativity, coordination, appreciation and spiritual and intellectual development.

INSTITUTE FOR
LOCAL SELF-RELIANCE
2425 18TH St., N.W.
Washington, D.C. 20009

A non-profit organization established in 1974, offers a new approach to urban planning. Helps cities and neighborhoods put their wealth to work, and then keep the benefits in their own neighborhoods. We analyze local economies, evaluate new technologies, and promote democratic decision-making, by showing residents how to plan their community and economic development.

We publish a variety of reports on self-reliance, solid waste management and community development. Send for free listing.

INTEGRITY INTERNATIONAL
PUBLISHING
P. O. Box 9
100 Mile House
B. C., Canada V0K 2E0

As the tides of change keep rising in our world, *Integrity International*, the journal of Emissary Foundation International plays an increasingly vital role, providing a balanced, penetrating perspective of what is happening, and highlighting creative endeavor wherever it occurs. Each issue covers a broad spectrum and introduces you to men and women all over the world whose concern is also for common sense and integrity in living.

We offer readers of this Guidebook a special opportunity to subscribe to *Integrity International* at the introductory rate of $18 for four (quarterly) issues (reg. $22, U.S.)

INTERNATIONAL
COMMUNES NETWORK
Communidad
Box 15128
10465 Stockholm
Sweden

It began with a festival at Laurieston Hall in Scotland in 1979, with over 100 people from 14 different countries. Since then there have been festivals and conferences in Denmark, Israel, Belgium and Scotland. Future festivals are planned.

In the past, whoever was organizing the next festival produced newsletters to keep people in touch with each other. Since the 1983 festival a regular quarterly bulletin has been set up, produced by Communidad.

The network is open to all communities who feel it has something for them (you choose us--we don't choose you). We publish a List which tells you who is active in

the Network. There is no fixed subscription, but a contribution is always appreciated.

LIGHT LIVING
Box 190-XYZ
Philomath, OR 97370

Distributors of the *1989 Guide to Unusual How-to Sources*. This guide describes 70 periodicals and handbooks on backyard tech, camping, crafts, finding new friends, gardening, home education, low-cost shelters, travel, woodslore, etc. All addresses are included. Free for SASE.

LOVING ALTERNATIVES
Calder Square
P. O. Box 10509
State College, PA 16805-0509

Loving Alternatives is a support and discussion group for those interested in multi-intimacy. There is no fee to join and visitors are welcome. We appreciate the opportunity to network, and we will keep your name and address in confidence. We do not schedule permissive events. The only requirements are a tolerance for other people's lifestyles and a belief in the desirability of an open mind.

We hold discussion groups weekly in the State College (Central Pennsylvania) area. We are trying to start similar groups in the Harrisburg and Philadelphia areas, and we are looking for regional contacts. Write for more information on our recommended reading list, list of nationwide referral sources, or our Central and Eastern Pennsylvania activities.

MERRIAM HILL CENTER
129 Raymond St.
Cambridge, MA 02140

Two facilities, one here, one in Greenville, NH. Learning Exchange programs available, including ones to Auroville (India), Findhorn (Scotland), and Arcosanti (Arizona). We offer "Orientation to Community", a week-long intensive residential program in Greenville for people interested in understanding the nature of community. Discussion, sharing, music, dance, theater and art, oriental and wholistic theory act as conceptual structures for the week. Visiting community members, students and others may stay from one to four months of reflective study of communities. Some "residents" do their own research and reading, others do projects designed by MHC staff. Write for further information.

NAROPA INSTITUTE
2130 Arapahoe Ave.
Boulder, CO 80302
(303) 444-0202

Est. '74 by Chogyam Trungpa, Rinpoche, Naropa Institute has developed an approach to education that joins intellect and intuition. This approach is based on appreciation of the discipline of both East and West with special influence from the Tibetan Buddhist tradition. Training in contemplative and meditative disciplines is available to interested students.

Attracts over 1,000 students each summer to over 200 courses and workshops in music, dance, psychology, martial arts, theater, visual arts, poetics, Buddhist studies and science. Year-round degree programs also. Intellect is trained through study and intuition through the practice of meditation and the arts, body awareness and movement.

Housing is usually available at nearby college residence halls at the University of Colorado, or at local apartment buildings.

Please write for info and schedules.

NATIONAL HISTORIC COMMUNAL SOCIETIES ASSOCIATION
Center for Communal Studies
University of Southern Indiana
8600 University Boulevard
Evansville, IN 47712

The NHCSA is an organization formed in 1975 to encourage the restoration, preservation, and public interpretation of the communitarian heritage and the study of communities, past and present. The Association carries out its work through a Center for Communal Studies, an interdisciplinary journal, *Communal Societies*, a newsletter, and two conferences annually. The Center at the University of Southern Indiana is the administrative office, clearinghouse for information, and archival research facility. Materials and artifacts from 90 historic communal groups and 325 contemporary communities are available. New acquisitions from historic and current communities are welcome. Write for memberships, subscriptions, and archival access.

NEW ALCHEMY INSTITUTE
237 Hatchville Rd.
East Falmouth, MA 02536

Small, not-for-profit research and education organization dedicated to the belief that humanity can and must live in a more gentle, environmentally sound manner. Goal--to devise new, productive ways to provide food, energy, shelter, and community design. Work in areas of agriculture, aquaculture, solar power, natural pest control, energy conservation and ecological modeling. Supported by private grants and contributions, gifts and dues from friends and 2,000 members. We are not a community in the usual sense of the word, not living here or together.

NEW LIFE FARM, INC.
Ozarks Resource Center
Brixey, MO 65618
(417) 679-4773

Distributors of the *Bioregional Bibliography* authorized by the North American Bioregional Congress. Compiled by members of the HBC, with assistance from bioregional groups and individuals from around the continent of Turtle Island, it is 46 pages long, lists all of the major books, periodicals, and articles associated with the bioregional movement in the last 15 years, and includes convenient sublistings for Basic Works, Directories, and Periodicals.

This is an essential research tool for activists, scholars, teachers, organizers, librarians, and anyone interested in one of the most important ecological movements of this century. Price is $4, including postage.

NEW ENGLAND NETWORK OF LIGHT
c/o Sirius Community
Baker Road
Shutesbury, MA 01072
(413) 259-1505

Directory listing 64 New Age communities, ashrams, cooperative businesses, wholistic health centers, magazines, etc. in New England and upstate New York. It includes 36 full-page descriptions contributed by each group about their center, with photos and graphics, and additional listings of groups in the back, along with other regional networks and directories (8 1/2 X 11). Write for current price.

PERMACULTURE INSTITUTE OF NORTH AMERICA
6488 S. Maxwelton Rd.
Clinton, WA 98236

Write for complete information.

RELOCATION RESEARCH/EMIGRANTS
P. O. Box 1122
Sierra Madre, CA 91024

National clearinghouse assisting individuals in planning a move from large urban areas to more livable environments (small towns and cities, islands, rural areas in general). Interested in not only intentional communities, but bioregions that embrace them, America's "small-town Shangri-las", survival retreats, last frontiers, regions of opportunity, etc.

Knowledgeable about myriad organizations and resource persons assisting in seeking personal Edens. Publish *Greener Pastures Gazette* and *Eden Seekers Guide*. Enclose SASE with specific request.

RITES OF PASSAGE, INC.
15 Hansen Rd.
Novato, CA 94947
(415)892-5371

A non-profit, non-sectarian, educational organization in Marin County, incorporated in 1977 by Steven and Meredith Foster, and is governed by a Board of not more than 12 directors. Offers courses which provide vision quest rite of passage experiences in a natural setting for youth and adults. The Vision Quest Training and Certification program was instituted in 1979 in response to the need to train practitioners in the various fields pertaining to human life transition. The staff are not therapists, shamans or healers. They are consultants, guides and friends. They offer a variety of tools from which the seeker creates, from personal experience, a meaningful rite of passage.

RURAL ALTERNATIVES
Box 122
Athens, OH 45701

A new service organization, uses work interest questionnaires to form cooperative work groups that will be the basis for new rural communities with private and common land. Free information or $5 for information, questionnaires, and enrollment. Send SASE to above address.

STELLE FOUNDATION, INC.
126 Sun St.
Stelle, IL 60919
(815)256-2252

Stelle Foundation, Inc. is an independent not-for-profit organization dedicated to personal, social, and global transformation. Our goal is to help individuals realize their full human potential by providing increased

access to various transformational programs. SFI programs and interest areas include SHARP, The Self-Help Association for the Realization of Potential, *Communities* magazine, and the Fellowship of Intentional Communities. Support is available to other transformational organizations through allocation of staff resources, funding and fundraising assistance, and consulting services in advertising and public relations. Please write or call for more information.

SUNBOW
15232 S.E. 364th
Auburn, WA 98002
(206) 939-8824 or 630-3569

Sunbow is a non-denominational community seeking to integrate our chosen spiritual paths with daily life. We are service oriented, Earth concerned and mostly non-residential, although some of us live in close proximity and there is a community house which can accommodate three members. We sponsor and host a variety of workshops and play days focused on spiritual unfoldment, Earth stewardship and fun! Our primary rhythm is a Sunday morning attunement and potluck country breakfast. All are welcome! Call for more info.

TRANSFORMATION TIMES
P. O. Box 425
Beavercreek, OR 97004
(513)632-7141

Transformation Times is a journal dedicated to expanding awareness of physical, mental and spiritual resources. We believe that an awareness of these resources will enable a transformation of planetary consciousness to one of Unity and Love. We gladly accept display ads, articles, classified ads, calendar information and other material that is in keeping with this intention. It is published monthly except for June and December. Write for more information. Subscriptions are $8/year. Sample copy $1.

TOUCHPOINT
P. O. Box 355
McVeytown, PA 17051
(717)899-7992

Open Relationships, Group Marriage, intimate friendship, multi-lateral marriage. Sound interesting? Touchpoint is a contact service for those who wish to develop long-term, emotionally as well as sexually intimate non-monogamous relationships. SASE for details. Sample $4.00.

WINDSTAR
Box 286
Snowmass, CO 81654

Windstar is located on 985 acres high in the Rocky Mountains, 18 miles from Aspen, CO. Our main building is heated by the sun and powered in part by alternative energy sources. Our one-acre bio-intensive garden, greenhouse and Bio-dome provide us with food, and we rejoice in our uniquely sublime climate, clean air, and good-natured staff.

Housing for participants is provided in two to five-person tipis furnished with platform beds and foam mattresses (you will need to bring a sleeping bag). Facilities include a wood-fired hot tub and sauna, a pond and solar showers and composting toilets.

Windstar offers educational programs in the fields of nutrition, education, and mind-body-spirit development. Topics range from energy conservation to world peace. Funded by John Denver, grants and donations. Programs are priced moderately to allow them to be self-sustaining. Scholarships are awarded on the basis of applicant's needs, funds and space available for that program.

Please write for more info and schedules.

WOMYN INTERESTED IN COMMUNITIES TOGETHER
Community Womyn
c/o Heathcote Center
21300 Heathcote Rd.
Freedom, MD 21053

A national conference for all womyn who are/were/or want to be living in womyn's communities is being envisioned within the next two years.

We would like to be in touch with womyn who would like to help dream, plan, organize and attend...and womyn who are living in or knowing of womyn's communities.

We envision this conference as a sharing, learning, networking, problem-solving, and potentially community farming time...affordable and accessible to all womyn.

We seek suggestions for the date and site, organizations, topics for discussion, name, etc.

WORLD FEDERATION OF SMALL URBAN GROUPS
P. O. Box 20341
Wichita, KS 67208
(316)686-7100

A few of us joined together recently to form a nonprofit organization called the World Federation of Small Urban Groups. The Federation is by intent an independent, world-wide network of small live-and-work-together groups dedicated to doing everything in their power to discover and provide as widely and deeply as they can the best possible conditions for the operation of what we call "the transformation process." This process is simply whatever it is that is always generating new understanding and appreciations between people, new ideas for constructive action, doing this by means of self-disclosure that risks rejection, disapproval, and misunderstanding and by means of an openness to new and different perspectives that risk seeing the world in a quite different way than ever before.

The transformative process is capable, we believe, of uniting all humanity in a common, trusting community, one willing to dispense with the use of reward and punishment as a way of resolving differences. We believe that it can save the world from self-destruction as nothing else can, to the extent that the great majority of people on earth today give it priority over every other concern.

We are looking for people to work with us, people who are at a turning point in their lives, who are ready and willing to make a radical turn in how they earn and spend money, where they live, with whom they socialize, and to what they give their ultimate commitment. We are, for the present, particularly interested in people who live in Kansas or the states surrounding it. If you qualify in the ways indicated, we would be delighted to have you write or phone us.

"Alternative Communities Today and Tomorrow"
June 6 - 15
with Corinne McLaughlin

This is a credit course offered through the University of Massachusetts (Anthropology 397A) exploring the innovative ideas being pioneered by these "research and development centers". Thirty New Age communities, including Findhorn, Sirius, High Wind, Chinook, Twin Oaks, Stelle, etc. Instructor is co-author of *Builders of the Dawn*, co-founder of Sirius Community and a former member of Findhorn. Held at Sirius, Baker Road, Shutesbury, MA 01072, (413) 259-1505. $245 for course, and $250 for accommodations and meals.

U.S. FEDERATION OF COOPERATIVE EDUCATION/ STRATEGY CENTERS

Members:
CLASPED HANDS
EDUCATION CENTER
P. O. Box 123
Etna, CA 96027
(916) 467-5397

RAINBOW RIDGE EDUCATION
AND PEACE CENTER
3689 Berea Rd.
Richmond, KY 40475
(606) 623-0695

SISU/OLANA CO-OP
EDUCATION GUILD
Route 45
Pomona, NY 10917

In large measure the wide-spread growth of Co-ops in Europe, Scandinavia and Britain has been due to their "Co-op Colleges" and "Educational Centers". In 1937, Rochdale Institute was established as their counter part in the U.S. It flourished on the national scene until 1952, thereafter, serving primarily the New York area.

In the meantime, regional co-ops, universities and several national co-op organizations have conducted programs of various kinds, mostly involving "skill" training. There has been a void--no place where people could immerse themselves in and soak up the philosophy of the movement, learn about its progress, its struggles, its progress, its implications--going away with a commitment to develop cooperative life patterns and a cooperative society.

So...in the mid-70's a small group of old/new co-op folk began to look at this need and decided that the country, as large as it is, did not need a single "College" or "Center", but many of them - simple facilities, low overhead, informal setting for seminars, etc. They all agreed there was a great need. Something" should be done about it!

These centers offer programs which focus on: review of history, philosophy, organization and operations of co-ops from Rochdale to present, including motivations and theoretical directions; consideration of strategies by which cooperative economic institutions can "successfully" replace competitive economic institutions. Faculty: individuals with long experience in various types and levels of co-op development, drawn from old and new wave co-ops. Learning in a "Folk School" context: including group participation, books, field trips, learning tailored to need/interest. Pace relaxed: time for cognition, meditation, dreaming. Contact any of these centers for more information and schedules.

Books, Etc.

ALTERNATIVE ACCESS DIRECTORY
P.O. Box 462
Kentfield, CA 94909

Periodicals, newspapers, and contacts for alternative resources including radio, communities, social change, bodywork, videos, cooperatives, publishing, and more. $8.95

ALTERNATIVE AMERICA
Box 1067 Harvard Square
Cambridge, MA 02238-1067
(617) 825-8895

Directory of 12,000+ alternative, progressive, innovative, experimental groups and organizations.

ALTERNATIVE MATERIALS IN LIBRARIES
P.O. Box 656
Metuchen, NJ 08840
(201) 548-8600

Handbook for librarians and others on buying small press publications. $16

APPOPRIATE COMMUNITY TECHNOLOGIES SOURCEBOOK
1110 - 6th St. NW, #300
Washington, DC 20001

Organizations, publications, professionals for community technologies including health, birthing, children, schools, homesteading, copperatives, and more. $3

COMMUNITIES MAGAZINE
Box 170
Stelle, IL 60919
(815) 256-2252

Reports on intentional communities and copperative organizations and resources. Directory of intentional communities.

COUNTERPART
Rt. 1, Box 375
Winthrop, WA 98862
(509) 996-2894

Support system for growing families in Eastern Washington. Monthly seminars on health and related issues.

GUIDE TO COMMUNITY MEDIA
121 Fulton St, 5th Fl
New York, NY 10038
(212) 619-3455

Advice on videos, films and slides on environmental and community issues, including social problems. Published by Media Network. $2.50

NEW AGE COMMUNITIES SLIDESHOW
Sirius Publishing
Baker Rd.
Shutesbury, MA 01072
(413) 259-1505

Produced by Corinne McLaughlin and Gordon Davidson, co-founders of Sirius Community and former college faculty members of the Findhorn Foundation in Scotland. They have taught classes in social change at Hampshire and Boston Colleges and American University. This slideshow was created from their travels around the U.S. to these various communities.

Today's communities are one of the mapmakers for humanity's journey into the future. They function as research and development centers for society, pioneering new solutions to old problems. This slideshow surveys 30 New Age communities around the country and the world which have created successful models of solar energy, wholistic health, worker-owned businesses, organic agriculture, and new conflict resolution techniques.

Rental: $50/wk., plus $50 refundable deposit. (140 slides, tape and script.) Sale: $220. (45-minute version.)

12-minute version, 77 slides, tape and script: $35/wk., plus $50 refundable deposit. Sale: $125

Video version: 45 minutes, Sale: $20, Rental: $10

BUILDERS OF THE NEW DAWN--COMMUNITY LIFESTYLES IN A CHANGING WORLD
by Corinne McLaughlin/Gordon Davidson

Communities have a new look, a new maturity and a new viability. Today's communities can be seen as blueprints for humanity's journey into the future...pioneering positive responses to global problems.

Builders of the New Dawn presents an overview of communities. It offers workable guidelines for building communities based on the experience of many community founders such as Peter and Eileen Caddy, Swami Kriyananda, Stephen Gaskin, Sun Bear, and Ken Keyes. The benefits and problems of community living are explored in depth, as well as innovative approaches to governance, economics, relationships, and spirituality being pioneered in today's communities. A resource listing of the 100 communities mentioned in the book is included with over 120 photos. An important value of this book is its insiders' view of communities, as the authors have lived in communities for over 23 years between them and have co-founded a community themselves.

Published by Sirius Publishing, distributed by New Leaf and Book People. Also available from Sirius Publishing. $12.95, plus $1.50 postage and packaging.

*THE BEST INVESTMENT:
Land in a Loving Community
by David Felder.

Shows how you can own a home without the bank owning you via intentional community. Discusses covenants and restrictions, financing your purchase, living well on less community dynamics, and illustrates its points with personal experience from the author's community. (Wellington) Paper. List: $8.50

*COMMUNITY IS POSSIBLE: Repairing
America's Roots
by Harry C. Boyte

The author of *The Backyard Revolution* explores how people have created, and still can create, community. You can do it anywhere, and it's needed everywhere. A read about it, then do it book. (Harper and Row) Paper. List: $6.95

*DESIGN WITH NATURE
by Ian L. McHarg
The basic design process for creating an ecologically-sound community within natural limits and intrinsic suitablilities begins with this invaluable guide to site selection. Before you decide where to build, read this. (Doubleday) List: $17.95

*A PATTERN LANGUAGE
by Christopher Alexander

A framework for community involvement in the construction of everything from workspaces and rooms to towns. *CoEvolution* says "in terms of brillance and universal usefulness, this is the best book we've ever reviewed." (Oxford) List: $45.00

*These books are available at a below-list discounted price. For more info on these and a complete listing of all their discounted books contact: Fred Ure, Better Lives for a Better World, P.O. Box 569, Cottage Grove, OR 97424.

The following books are available from Community Service Books, P.O. Box 243, Yellow Springs, OH 45387 (513) 767-2161. Please write them for a complete book list, prices and order form.

THE NEW CONSCIOUSNESS SOURCEBOOK

Spiritual Community Guide No. 6. Features information and addresses of thousands of new age centers, schools and businesses. Health, meditation, therapy, bodywork, movement, occult, nutrition and more....Articles and illustrations.

"Within the Grace-full bounty of the book you can find some form which may be right for you at this moment."- -Ram Dass. $8.95.

Send check or money order to K.R.I. Publications, P.O. Box 1550C, Pomona, CA 91769. Include $1.50 shipping and handling. (CA residents add 6% sales tax.) Also, write to above address for FREE CATALOG of over 150 new age books and tapes.

NEW ORGANIZATIONAL PROSPECTS FOR COMMUNITY AND CONSERVATION LAND TRUSTS
by Greg Galbraith

An excellent legal study of the model for a regional land trust network. Hawk Hill Community Land Trust is featured to explain the legal documents. This is an original study designed to assist the formtion of other land trusts. Ozark Regional Land Trust. A valuable manual.

1984. 16 pgs text/40 documents. $10.00.

THE SMALL COMMUNITY: Foundation of Democratic Life
by Arthur E. Morgan

First published in 1942, this book is Arthur Morgan's definitive work on the significance and potentials of the small community. As relevant and inspiring today as when it was written. The essence of the Community Service philosophy. 1984. 336 pp.

SEEDS OF TOMORROW:
Communities That Work
by Oliver and Chris Popenoe

A study of 21 intentional communities on five continents and in eight different countries. The authors are concerned with "how they came to be, what they believe, how they live, how they support themselves, how membership is determined, and how they relate to the world around them." Harper and Row. 1984. 310 pp.

TAKING CHARGE OF OUR LIVES:
Living Responsibly in the World
by American Friends Service Committee, San Francisco.

A how-to-do-it for simple living and personal and social change. Harper and Row. 1984. 254 pp.

PARTNERING: A Guide to Co-Owning Anything from Homes to Home Computers
by Lois Rosenthal

An extremely readable book full of commonsense advice designed to help anyone everyone partner or co-own anything and everything from gerbils to condominiums. Provides a questionnaire to match up partners and sample contracts and agreements. Writers Digest Books. 1983. 358 pp.

COMMUNITY DREAMS: Ideas for Enriching Neighborhood and Community
by Bill Berkowitz

Creative, practical ideas, small in scale and low in cost, for improving community life. Culled from the author's and his friend's imagination and experience. Ideas range from eminently sensible to delightfully whimsical. Impact Publishers. 1984. 225 pp.

EMPLOYEE OWNERSHIP: Issues, Resources, and Legislation
by Corey Rosen

A thought-provoking and well-documented handbook on employee ownership. Supplies a general background on the subject plus offers suggestions for possible legislation. National Center for Employee Ownership. 1982. 82 pp.

THE BACKYARD REVOLUTION:
Understanding the New Citizen Movement
by Harry C. Boyte

Interesting, informative and well-researched book about the new social movement that emerged in the '70's and is characterized as a form of grassroots activism that showed people taking action for themselves to remedy problems in their lives. Valuable appendixes that list support networks for community organizing. Temple University Press. 1980. 271 pp.

THE GROUP HOUSE HANDBOOK
by Nancy Brandwein, Jill MacNeice and Peter Spiers

A book for preventing "If only I had known what I was getting into..." Frank discussion of advantages and disadvantages of group house living. Very entertaining. Acropolis Books. 1982. 254 pp.

CELERY WINE:
Story of a Country Commune
by Elaine Sundancer

Narrative account of the building of a rural commune by disenchanted city folk. Nice evolution and feeling. 1973. 176 pp.

THE COMMUNITY LAND TRUST HANDBOOK
by Institute for Community Economics

A Definitive and up-to-date guide to forming community land trusts with actual case studies and legal documents. Practical strategies to protect forests and farmland, redevelop rundown urban neighborhoods, and encourage the construction of quality, low-income housing. The Institute for Community Economics. 1982. 230 pp.

A COMPENDIUM OF LAND TRUST DOCUMENTS
Compiled by Herb Goldstein - 1976.
Community Service Reprint - 1981.

A useful aid for those writing a Community Land Trust agreement, with examples from a variety of existing agreements. 37 pp.

SCHOOL FOR THE YOUNG
by Warren Stetzel

Changing conditions demand education for a new consciousness. This is an engaging report on the thoughts of an experienced teacher, now a member of Raven Rocks community. Both entertaining and inspirational. Raven Rocks Publishing. 1977. 224 pp.

THE COMMUNITY OF THE FUTURE AND THE FUTURE OF COMMUNITY
by Arthur Morgan

A view of community potential and its aspects. Suggestions for community improvement are made: cooperation between communities, local government, economic life, recreation, religion, intentional communities. 1957. 166 pp.

INDUSTRIES FOR SMALL COMMUNITIES
by Arthur E. Morgan

An economic base can be developed for small communities without depending on big industry. A description of how this was done in Yellow Springs, Ohio. 1953. 107 pp.

Index of
Communities

Index of Communities

NEW FROM HARBIN SPRINGS PUBLISHING

BODYWORK TANTRA:
On Land and In Water

Imagine yourself being floated in a naturally-heated warm pool...a gentle rocking, gradually stretching you from side to side, rolling your spine looser and looser as you are swirled through the water.

Harold Dull, international teacher, author, and Director of the School of Shiatsu and Massage here at Harbin Hot Springs shares his revolutionary new system of massage in this excellent book. This new form of bodywork takes on new dimensions with both giver and receiver experiencing a greater opening and nurturing from the heart.

8 1/2" x 10 5/8", 112 pages, Paper, $10.95 ISBN 0-944202-00-4

EUREKA!
The Six Stages of Creativity

There is nothing mysterious about human creativity. Scientific and artistic inspiration, religious revelation, and the ideas and insights produced routinely by what we call "intuition" are natural phenomena.

In this amazing book Ross Smith takes us on a journey into our own creative potential, describing each stage of the process by which our left and right brain hemispheres interact to create achievements so extraordinary our logical left brain believes them to be miraculous in origin. A wonderful gift for a friend or loved one.

8 1/2" X 11", 172 pages, Paper, $11.95 ISBN 0-944202-02-0

THE NEW AGE COMMUNITY GUIDEBOOK

Explore the world of alternative lifestyle, intentional communities with this handy guide which includes listings for over 200 communities, including names, addresses and descriptions of each (rural, urban, religious, Canadian and foreign). The guidebook also has a section on New Age and Educational Centers, books, articles and information relevant to community living. This book is a MUST for anyone interested in joining a community. This publication was originally created by the Community Referral Service.

8 1/2" X 11", 128 pages, Paper, $7.95, ISBN 0-944202-03-9

✂

SHIP TO:

First Name: _____ Last Name: _____

Street Address: _____ Apt. #: _____

City: _____ State: _____ Zipcode: _____

Qty.	Book Title	Price Each	Total Price

Subtotal	
Sales Tax	
Shipping	
TOTAL	

California Residents add 6% tax.

Shipping & Handling: Add $1.50 for one book; $2.50 for 2-5 books; $3.50 for 6-10 books.

Make your check or money order payable to Harbin Springs Publishing and mail to: P. O. Box 82, Middletown, CA 95461.